EVERYDAY LEADERSHIP

I0105079

This engaging book presents useful frameworks, key ideas, and practical techniques – all grounded in scientific research – to help you lead better on a day-to-day basis.

Whether you are moving into your first leadership role or are already a leader and looking to expand your purview and skillset, this is an essential resource for understanding leadership. Recognizing that a one-size-fits-all leadership approach isn't possible, *Everyday Leadership* encourages you to develop your own leader mindset. It gives a foundational overview of what leadership is, what makes leaders effective, and how to think systematically about organizations and teams. Translating science into accessible and practical language, it also offers general guidance for those who are interested in expanding their skills and knowledge. These teachings are supported by easy-to-follow reflective questions and exercises, allowing you to put these ideas into practice and develop a leadership practice that works best for you. At a time when people need to be empowered to lead, it will encourage you to truly think about what it means to lead other people in work and in life.

Providing a toolkit that covers basic theories, concepts, and practices in leadership research, this book is a go-to resource for all leaders wherever you are in your leadership journey.

Ross Blankenship, PhD, is an organizational psychologist, executive coach, and a lecturer at the University of Virginia, USA. He is the founder of the leadership coaching and consulting firm Tuesday Advisors, and author of *Assessing CEOs and Senior Leaders*. Learn more about his work at rossblankenship.io.

"*Everyday Leadership* offers a fresh, accessible perspective on leadership that resonates deeply in today's ever-changing workplace. Blankenship invites readers to reimagine leadership through the lens of daily actions, empowering them to develop a personalized approach to leading. This concise guide serves as an ideal meditation for anyone transitioning into a leadership role, providing practical tools to navigate this shift with confidence and clarity. A must-read for aspiring and experienced leaders alike."

Dr. Marshall Goldsmith, *Thinkers50 #1 Executive Coach and* New York Times *bestselling author of* The Earned Life, Triggers *and* What Got You Here Won't Get You There

"*Everyday Leadership* is a concise, thought-provoking guide to the identity of a leader. Read this book to better formulate your leadership self-concept and lead with confidence as a result."

Richard Davis, PhD, *Author of* Good Judgment *and* Intangibles of Leadership

"A meditation on leadership that will help readers develop a personal understanding of how to lead in their own context, *Everyday Leadership* is a must read both for leaders and for the coaches who support them."

Alex Pascal, PhD, *Founder and CEO of Coaching.com*

"Effective leadership occurs through the culmination of actions and decisions that leaders make every single day. In *Everyday Leadership,* Ross Blankenship breaks down the act of being a leader into approachable, logical, and thought-provoking steps, while also normalizing many of the challenges and feelings of self-doubt that leaders face. This book is a great resource for developing leaders at all stages of their leadership journey."

Brodie Riordan, PhD, *Author of* The Coaching Shift *and* Feedback Fundamentals

"Ross Blankenship provides a safe, conversational space for people – regardless of experience, confidence, or tenure – to build a mental map of what leadership could look like translated through their own experience, personality, and values.

He provides structure without the rigidity of typical leadership dogma and practical, real-world examples that help you see yourself in the lessons. I will refer this book to anyone looking to prepare for a leadership role or to uplevel their current leadership practice."

Maggie Sass, PhD, *EVP of Content, Research and Professional Services, TalentsmartEQ*

"*Everyday Leadership* is a testament to the fact that leadership is about your practices more than your position. Unlike most leadership books that offer one-size-fits-all maps to navigate the evolving world of work, *Everyday Leadership* will help you develop a compass that you can apply to whatever environment you find yourself in. This book will help you grow."

Simone Stolzoff, *Author of* The Good Enough Job

EVERYDAY LEADERSHIP

A GUIDE TO DEVELOPING YOUR MINDSET AS A LEADER

Ross Blankenship

R Routledge
Taylor & Francis Group

NEW YORK AND LONDON

Cover design by Garrett Cummings. Photo by Olivier Depaep on Unsplash.

First published 2025
by Routledge
605 Third Avenue, New York, NY 10158

and by Routledge
4 Park Square, Milton Park, Abingdon, Oxon, OX14 4RN

Routledge is an imprint of the Taylor & Francis Group, an informa business

Library of Congress Cataloging-in-Publication Data
Names: Blankenship, J. Ross, author.
Title: Everyday leadership : a guide to developing your mindset as a leader / Ross Blankenship.
Description: New York, NY : Routledge, 2025. | Includes bibliographical references and index.
Identifiers: LCCN 2024032728 (print) | LCCN 2024032729 (ebook) | ISBN 9781032616223 (hardback) | ISBN 9781032607856 (paperback) | ISBN 9781032616193 (ebook)
Subjects: LCSH: Leadership.
Classification: LCC BF637.L4 B53 2025 (print) | LCC BF637.L4 (ebook) | DDC 158/.4--dc23/eng/20240821
LC record available at https://lccn.loc.gov/2024032728
LC ebook record available at https://lccn.loc.gov/2024032729

ISBN: 978-1-032-61622-3 (hbk)
ISBN: 978-1-032-60785-6 (pbk)
ISBN: 978-1-032-61619-3 (ebk)

DOI: 10.4324/9781032616193

Typeset in Palatino and Scala Sans
by KnowledgeWorks Global Ltd.

Dedication

For all those seeking to lead better.
&
For my mom and dad, who continue to encourage
me to learn and to write.

Contents

About the author   x
Acknowledgments   xi

Introduction: Who you are is how you lead   1

1   What we talk about when we talk about leadership   11

2   What a leader does   25

3   How the task of leadership evolves   39

4   Learning how you practice leadership   47

5   What are you trying to accomplish?   59

6   What do you owe the people you lead?   70

Afterword: Now what?   79
Workbook: Putting the book to work   81
Index   114

About the author

Ross Blankenship is an organizational psychologist, leadership coach, and consultant. As the founder and principal of Tuesday Advisors, he works with a wide array of leaders and leadership teams to enhance performance, communication, and decision-making. He also partners with organizations to conduct in-depth succession planning, leadership development, and executive assessment projects. His first book *Assessing CEOs and Senior Leaders: A Primer for Consultants* was published by the American Psychological Association in 2021, and he regularly writes a newsletter on navigating complex decisions in work, leadership, life, and career called "Now What?" He holds a B.A. in English language and literature from the University of Virginia and an M.S. and PhD in consulting psychology from the California School of Professional Psychology. He and his wife live in Birmingham, AL, with their two daughters and two dogs. Learn more at rossblankenship.io.

A NOTE ABOUT EXAMPLES

All anecdotes and vignettes in the text are reflective of actual conversations and experiences, though details have been changed to preserve anonymity.

Acknowledgments

I'm grateful for the opportunity to write a book about this topic which I find continually interesting and urgent. Thank you to the team at Routledge/Taylor & Francis, especially Zoe Thomson-Kemp, who believed in this idea from the first read, and Maddie Gray for her patient support. Thank you to Jon Yarian for the engaging conversations and insights that have helped shape the ideas and tone of this book. Thanks to Sarah Parcak for giving me the nudge I needed right when I needed it and for insisting that I keep going. Sarah also introduced me to Michael Signorelli, whose sure-eyed editorial guidance and gracious feedback helped me learn how to write a better book. To my early readers, thank you for your input and insight, especially Garrett Cummings, Kammie Kasten, and Maggie Sass. Thanks also to Garrett for the sharp cover design. Thanks to Dan Sartor for doing his best to keep me sane throughout the writing process. Thanks to my loving family for the support, and to my daughters – Sugar Bear and Lu Bug – for continually reminding me that my work is only a part of my life. And with deepest gratitude, thank you to my wife, Din, for her steadfast love and encouragement, as ever.

Introduction

Who you are is how you lead

If you're reading this book, you're probably going through a transition of some kind in your work.

Maybe you've been promoted into a role that requires you to formally manage other people for the first time, or maybe you're stepping into a new role that requires you to expand the scope and scale of your leadership. Maybe you're feeling a latent sense of anxiety about the transition. Maybe you feel like a fraud being on a leadership team or thinking of yourself as a "leader" at all and you're looking for a way out of the vicious spiral of imposter syndrome. Or perhaps you're simply still working out for yourself what it means for you to lead others in a way that feels substantive and sustainable and true to yourself.

If you find yourself in a transition of this kind, I say *good*. This is what you wanted. This is the position in which you can learn most about how you lead. You're right where you need to be to learn, adapt, and grow.

Here's a good place to start: What changes when you "become a leader?"

Well, nothing really. You may be "a leader," but you're still you. It doesn't mean you're a new person, or that you need to become more intense or authoritative. It doesn't mean you need to become more sociable or more intelligent, or that you need to have all the answers or even know exactly what you're doing.

Perhaps your title changes. Likely the responsibilities and requirements of your job expand. The things you'll need to

DOI: 10.4324/9781032616193-1

be thinking about may shift, whether that's made clear to you by other people or not.

You may start to be viewed differently by the people you work with. You may now be "boss" to them, and they may start trying to manage your perception of them. People may start taking what you say more explicitly, which may mean you need to be more careful about what you say and how you interact with others. It may land differently now when you joke, ask questions, hypothesize, and share your anxieties and fears.

Your job may now require you to make decisions on behalf of other people: what they do, how they should do it, and why they should do it. And all the while you may be wondering, "Wait, am I doing any of this right? Am I thinking about this right? Am I really a leader?"

FEELING VERSUS DOING

Here's the thing, you will almost certainly be required to do the stuff of leadership before you feel like a leader. Though your role may have changed or expanded, almost certainly no one has sat down with you to say, "Congratulations, you're still you, you got promoted because you were good at your job, but now your job is different and has become more complex and a bit less straightforward."

This happens because we make a few assumptions about people as they move through organizations. High performers get promoted because they're good at their jobs. The assumption is they were good at *that*, they'll be good at *this*.

But *this* is a different type of job. There tends to be a perception that leading and managing others is largely characterized by "soft skills" and that those skills are easy to pick up naturally. This assumption ignores the fact that "soft skills" are precisely the skills required to work effectively with other people and that those skills can be quite complex, abstract, and emotionally demanding. And it's not as if everything stops so you can get up to speed with what's new and different about your role. You may ask, "What should I be doing?" And hear back, "We hired *you* to figure it out!"

And all this learning must occur in the context of continuing to do your job. As a result, when you get promoted, you immediately feel overwhelmed. There's too much to learn. There are new relationships to form and new ways of interacting with the people around you, and it feels like there is no time to reflect and try to wrap your mind around it all. It's like trying to change clothes while running.

A lot of the stress of this transition simply comes from the mindset shift that's required to adapt to a new way of thinking about yourself and your work, essentially answering the question, "Yes, but how do *I* lead?"

YOU ARE WHERE YOU ARE

Whether you're in your first leadership role or a role that requires you to expand the scope and scale of your leadership capability, this transition requires you to evolve, integrating who you are now with who you need to become to meet the demands of the challenge in front of you. Add to this the fact that you were likely never explicitly taught about leadership or how to think about yourself as a leader, and you have perfectly good cause to wonder what exactly it is you're supposed to be doing now that you're "leading."

And this challenge persists over time because the task of leadership continually changes as you change and as people and organizations change around you. Take a simple example: Delegating a task to an individual contributor may require a different way of communicating than delegating to someone who manages individual contributors, and yet another way of communicating for someone managing managers. Moving up in an organization frequently requires thinking further into the future, adapting to changing cultural dynamics, and relying more on collaboration and influence to get things done.

The solution to this challenge is to reframe the way we think about leadership and how it's done. Thinking about it not as the grand gestures, risks, and achievements that characterize our cultural archetypes of what it means to lead, but as ordinary everyday moments.

At the fundamental level, leadership is a relationship with other people, and it is a form of interaction that is accessible to anyone. This framing opens the possibility that leadership happens all the time between and among all kinds of people; that the repeated gestures in our relationships, the practices of communication and collaboration and effort we return to on a daily basis have more to say about how we lead than our grandest theories.

In this way, our perception of leadership – what it is, what it means, and how it can be done – is so intimately tied to who we are and how we view the world around us that, to a certain extent, we must each develop our own individual theory of leadership. Leadership is so personal that anyone who seeks to understand it in the context of their own life must necessarily begin with autobiography.

A LITTLE BIT ABOUT ME

I am the son of a psychotherapist mother and a consulting psychologist father. I grew up in a house where talking about work meant talking about people.

I'm sure I didn't quite understand what my parents did while I was growing up, but I knew that I heard a lot about what other people did, from the motivations and successes of business leaders and entrepreneurs to the stresses and struggles of people's everyday lives. The refrain of my childhood seemed to be: *I met the most interesting person at work today.*

I could understand why people would talk to a therapist to process the complex emotions and challenges that emerge in life, but it was never quite clear to me why a business leader would need the same type of outlet in the form of executive coaching. That is, until I got my first job out of college.

A tale of two bosses

In my early 20s, I worked at a fast-growing company during and after the 2008 financial crisis. The group I was hired into was expanding, and they were knocking down walls on our floor to accommodate new people. I was hired into an analyst role, but I worked on special projects for both my immediate boss and the head of the group. It was an odd setup that gave me unique insight into how the group was being managed, and it became a case study for me on how leadership impacts people's lives.

The head of the group never seemed to really be listening when I spoke to him. He was always trying to do two or more things at the same time. I couldn't tell if he was moving as fast as he could to seize the opportunities before him, or if he was just holding on for dear life. He made simple mistakes, his drive to move fast made him inefficient, and his logic was circuitous at times. I remember thinking he always seemed to be sweating in his pinstripe suit, pushing his damp hair up off his forehead while he tried to communicate something about the strategy of our group. This pace led to a lack of attentiveness, and his chaotic presence left us all to wonder what exactly he was working on and what he was thinking.

My immediate boss led in such a different way that the comparison was jarring. He was intentional about listening to people and hearing them out. He seemed to want to make sure that he not only heard what people had to say but that they *felt heard* by him. It seemed like his primary job shifted from whatever his mandate had been to simply running air cover for the team, based on how the group was being led. I remember thinking it must have been impossible for him to get anything done beyond just talking with people on the team. At times, I felt guilty about how much of his day he would spend talking to me, helping me learn.

It was a time of tumult; it was a time of growth. As new people joined the team, account assignments had to shift to make sure the right people with the most relevant expertise were selling to the right clients. Bigger accounts yielded bigger commissions, so there was a naturally competitive nature to the assignment process. My job was to help my immediate boss to figure out the right market segmentation, assign sales coverage, and try to communicate changes to the team in a way that didn't make everyone angry. When he had to take an account from someone, he made time to sit with them in his office and revisit the broader strategy we were working toward in a personal way, laying out the path he saw for that person's participation in the overall growth of the group. While this re-assignment process resulted in some disappointment, his approach also helped to emphasize a common group identity and fostered some appreciation that he wasn't making decisions on a whim, that he was doing the best he could to consider the overall impact on the team.

On occasion though, the head of the group would step in, make an executive decision to re-assign a key account to a favored salesperson, or reorganize how accounts were assigned in the first place, and the whole process would derail and start again. Over time, the tension between these two leadership styles created an environment in which it was never quite clear what the overarching strategy was or where any individual position fit within it.

This created some uncertainty, and thereby anxiety, around how individual leadership decisions would affect team members' livelihoods in the short and long term. Those who were in favor got the best accounts which could lead to life-changing transactions, a new car by the end of the week, a new house by the end of the month. Those who were not in favor continually had their accounts reshuffled. As their trust in leadership dwindled, their performance seemed to degrade along with their ability to support their families.

Turnover was a common occurrence, and frequently when people left the company, they wound up leaving the industry as well.

Experiencing the disorganization and in-fighting that can occur in a business with dysfunctional leadership helped me understand that leadership is not just about how a person shapes the fate of an organization, but also about how a person in a position of power or influence or authority impacts other people's lives in incredibly direct and long-lasting ways.

It was this job, experiencing and observing the dramatic impact that different types of leadership can have on people, which made me want to go to graduate school and study leadership and psychology.

So, I got a PhD in consulting psychology, a field that sits at the intersection of organizational and counseling psychology. I wanted to learn what causes some leaders to infuse positivity into an environment – to help others broaden and build their awareness, understanding, and capacities – and what causes others to inject negativity into an environment, increasing feelings of anxiety, frustration, and diminished capacity. I wanted to learn what makes someone good at leading, and I wanted to help people get better at that work.

What I do now

I've spent the past decade researching and writing about leadership, coaching leaders, and consulting to organizations of all types and sizes. I've assessed hundreds of executives for selection, development, and succession planning, work that I wrote about in my first book, *Assessing CEOs and Senior Leaders: A Primer for Consultants*. And I've spent much of my time coaching founders and executives one-on-one, helping them to navigate the complex dynamics and decisions that emerge in their roles leading others.

While doing this work, I've often been in the position to recommend books about leadership, work, and career decision-making. I am most frequently asked what to read by people who are taking on roles that require new or expanded ways of thinking about what leadership is and how to do it. But when they ask me what they should read, I find myself recommending books with a caveat: "This is *one way* to think about leadership," "This describes *an approach* to leading other people," or "Just take what this book says about CEOs and try to apply it to your own role."

I do this because most books about leadership seem to rely on extreme frameworks and ways of thinking. They all seem to be full of imperatives – *do this, don't do that* – which only become harder to adhere to the more frequent and urgent the demands become.

It's as if these books have been written for some future idealized version of myself. *Ross the Leader*. He'll be radically candid when it counts, he'll embody the seven habits of highly effective people, he'll know the 21 irrefutable laws of leadership by heart, start with why, and manage teams of teams with extreme ownership. He'll be incredible, Ross the Leader, off in his imminently capable future state where he has acquired all the perfect knowledge, awareness, and insight necessary for him to dare to lead others.

Except of course he won't. Because no amount of knowledge can substitute the fact that knowledge must be applied. Whether I've learned a new fact or an interesting method matters less than my ability to do something with it. And this is especially the case when it comes to leading, where the people and context and limitations of my present circumstances are all deeply relevant to what I can do and to what effect.

WHAT'S IN THE BOOK

The structure of this book is based on a simple premise: thinking of yourself as a leader, or perhaps just as someone who can lead, requires you to consider and acknowledge a few things about leadership and about yourself. First, it requires thinking more clearly about leadership itself, what it is and what it aims to accomplish.

Chapter 1, *What We Talk about When We Talk about Leadership,* explores our cultural perceptions of leadership, our preconceived notions, and how our individual experiences shape what we think about leaders and leading.

Chapter 2, *What a Leader Does,* aims to get beneath these preconceived notions and perceptions and provide some perspective on what is actually happening when leadership is occurring. This is where we zoom into everyday interactions and the kinds of behavior that characterize leadership.

Chapter 3 describes *How the Task of Leadership Evolves.* This chapter aims to broaden the aperture a bit and provide a sense for the ways in which the work of leading changes as you move up in a hierarchy and the scope of your influence expands.

Chapter 4 presents an exploration of *Learning How You Practice Leadership* in which you can start thinking about yourself specifically, your natural tendencies, strengths, weaknesses, values, and behavior, and how those may interact with the environment in which you intend to lead.

There is an underlying belief infused into all my thinking and writing and coaching and consulting, and it is basically this, questions about work are questions about life. Work decisions are life decisions. Work anxiety is life anxiety. Work crises are life crises. This is easy to forget, easy to gloss over, as we make our way through our daily activities. But when you are wrestling with what to make of your work, what to make of the position you've found yourself in, and what kind of impact you can have on the people around you, you are ultimately wrestling with what all this work amounts to in the end.

Chapter 5 moves beyond who you are and what context you find yourself in and directly asks the question – *What Are You Trying to Accomplish?* How you think about your work generally, your career, your goals, and your motives is directly relevant to how you show up as a leader. This chapter pushes you to take a clear-eyed look at why you do what you do, how you make decisions about your work, and what you're hoping to achieve.

Chapter 6, *What Do You Owe the People You Lead?*, zooms all the way out to consider the idea that leadership is ultimately about legacy and that our legacy is most readily shaped by our everyday actions.

HOW TO USE THE BOOK

As you may be able to tell, this is an atypical leadership book. It is not an exhortation, which is common in the genre. It is not a point-by-point how-to. If you're looking for a list of five things to do to lead better, if you're hoping to find a method that always works, if you are hunting for absolute certainty, I'm sorry to disappoint.

Instead, this book aims to till the soil of your thinking, to rattle the cage *just a little bit* on your perception of leadership, what it is and what it does. If you're interested in that, in learning, and re-energizing how you think about the practice of leadership; if you're interested in expanding your identity as a leader and asking new questions of yourself, keep going.

CHAPTER 1

What we talk about when we talk about leadership

When we talk about leadership, we don't talk about any one thing, we talk about everything.

We talk about the political landscapes of countries and states and cities and municipalities; we talk about business and sports and nonprofits and community groups; we talk about adventure, ingenuity, risk, inspiration, and dedication to the cause; we talk about the highest aims of the human spirit and the evilest expressions; we talk about hopes and dreams and visions for the future.

When we talk about leadership, what we talk about is life, death, and all manners of human relationships. This can make our conversations about leadership interesting and inspiring, but it can also make it hard to talk about how to *do* leadership. The more we talk about the various expressions of leadership, the harder it becomes to talk about the mechanisms that make it work. In addition, we can all provide our own definitions of leadership – examples, outcomes we've observed, lists of traits we admire – because we all have preconceived notions of what leadership is and how it should be done.

In fact, you already think about leadership in ways that you may not realize. Take a moment to try this exercise:

- When you think of the word "leader," who comes to your mind?
- What do leaders do?
- What do leaders *not* do?
- What does it mean to be leaderlike?
- What makes a leader great?

DOI: 10.4324/9781032616193-2

Feel free to just think about it, but it also may be useful to jot down a few ideas so you can come back to them later and see what you wrote.

MY OWN PRECONCEIVED NOTIONS

Who comes to mind for me

When I think of the word "leader," I think of the people who have shaped the course of my life in tangible ways. I think of people like my parents, a boss I had early in my career, a friend and mentor from my church, my internship supervisor from my early work as a consulting psychologist. I think of people who are (or have been) an active participant in my life, people with whom I've had meaningful relationships. So, part of my mental representation of a leader is of someone I know well, someone who isn't distant, and whom I perceive as thoughtful and concerned about my best interest.

What leaders do

In my mind, leaders are almost always thinking about the future, they are interpreting the present and how it relates to what has happened and what could happen. For one reason or another, I believe they can see and explain things that I cannot see or explain in the same way, and they are willing and able to share that perspective with me in a useful way. I also think of a leader as someone at a podium. Someone speaking and delivering an important message to a group of people; they are curious about the people around them and the world around them and how they might influence it for the better; they are willing to express their own humanity and vulnerability to bring people together.

What leaders don't do

I have this notion that leaders are almost never unwilling to interact with others. I don't exactly mean here that they're extroverted, but that they are able to be with other people, even when they may not want to be, in a way that creates a positive impact. A leader is almost never "off," which is to say they are always leading. Somewhere in my mind is the idea that "a leader is a leader," that someone *is* or *is not* a leader and once that has been established it doesn't change. I don't think it's true of course. But I think the notion is persistent because it makes it seem like leadership is something that can be revealed; that there is an amount of leadership knowledge or skill I can acquire, or that there's a certain type of experience I could have that would make known the leader within me, and somehow negate the fact that I am still a flawed human being. For better or worse, I find myself thinking that a leader is *never* only interested in their own well-being.

What it means to be leaderlike

To me, being "leaderlike" means being influential. Having a voice or a perspective that is sought out. It means shaping perceptions and the course of events. Being in a room and having people sort of collectively turn and say, "Yeah, but what do they think?" The person they turn to – that person is leaderlike. It means being willing to assert a vision of what's possible or what could be, helping align others toward that vision, and enabling them to get there. Being leaderlike means caring about other people, what happens to them, and how you might take action to shape those outcomes for the better.

What makes a leader great

I think adding the idea of "greatness" to this exercise is useful for a couple of reasons. I have a genuinely hard time answering this question for myself. Greatness implies some sense of grandeur that I think can be misleading. To some extent, I think the more we focus on the grand gesture, the more we miss the everyday. So, if people like Abraham Lincoln or Martin Luther King, Jr. come to mind as great leaders, I'm not exactly sure what specific characteristic or ability makes them great. Was it their ability to communicate in such impactful ways? Their ability to make sense of their complicated and fraught times in a way that brought people some sense of peace? All of those things? I'm also mindful that greatness is, like beauty, in the eye of the beholder.

What I view as great may be viewed as its opposite by someone with other interests and values. This is a long way of saying I suppose I'm not sure about what I think makes a leader great, except to say I think it probably has something to do with an ability to communicate effectively and in a way that inspires others.

But this is just me.

Did you try the exercise before reading my answer? What do you already believe about leadership? Did you find yourself nodding along with me in certain places or recognizing how your perceptions diverge from mine?

WHERE OUR LEADERSHIP BELIEFS COME FROM

Images, myths, and archetypes

Much of our thinking about leadership is driven by our belief that there are innate characteristics that make a person more or less adept at leading other people; that if you're not born with *the right stuff*, well, then you're out of luck when it comes to leading.

The traits that pop to mind in this line of thinking are all the stereotypical ones from a time gone by – tall, attractive, intelligent, ambitious, extroverted…male. This holdover from the "Great Man" theory of leadership suggests that leaders are born not made and that history is shaped by individuals.[1] That there are some who stand tall and confident and are able to withstand the limelight of leadership, and others who simply are not and cannot. Think of Napoleon riding up and down the line of his troops inspiring them to run to their demise by casting a vision of the glory of the empire, think of Winston Churchill broadcasting comforting words to a nation frightened by nightly bombardments.

When we think about leadership, we think about certain types of people from certain places with certain pedigrees. We think about people who stand out for one reason or another.

We assume the people who can lead are those who *seem* leaderlike, who are in positions of authority. Hell, we even call them "leadership positions." But is everyone who occupies such a position necessarily leading?

Crossed wires

In many circumstances, we conflate other social and psychological concepts with leadership. Leadership generates talk about positions and titles, traits and characteristics, knowledge, experience, competencies, and motivation. There are so many related concepts that we often struggle to define what exactly leadership is and what it isn't. For example, much has been made of the distinction between leadership and management,[2] but what about the distinction between leadership and other constructs like authority, power, charisma, need for achievement, resilience, teamwork, and followership (to name a few). In what ways do we differentiate the work of leadership from these other ideas?

They are tricky distinctions to make because our thinking about leadership tends to be informed by our preconceived notions about who should lead, how it should be done, and what it should accomplish; in short, they comprise our implicit theories of leadership.

Implicit leadership theories

Implicit leadership theories are our beliefs about what describes the prototypical leader.[3] Depending on where you grew up, the cultural influences that have shaped your life, and the people you admire, you may look for and appreciate different things about leadership behavior, both its positive and negative influences.

If you've experienced being led as being told what to do or being held to a demanding set of expectations with punishment as the consequence for failing to meet them, you may view leadership as all command and control. If you've experienced being led as being heard and encouraged, or being supported and given the resources to pursue your own goals, you may view leadership as all empowerment. Or perhaps you've had experiences such as these that led to negative consequences, and you've reacted against them. You experienced empowerment that led to a sense of overwhelming ambiguity, and so your notion of leadership pushes against that. All these interactions shape your perceptions of what it feels like to be led, what it should and shouldn't feel like, and what we think is happening when leadership is working and when it isn't.

We categorize people as "leaders" based on how well they line up with our beliefs about what leadership is.[4] What's interesting about these beliefs, though, is that they point to a common mistake we make in thinking about leadership. Implicit theories tend to be more indicative of who we think will make a good leader versus who might actually lead well.

It's a subtle distinction, but an important one. In thinking about leadership, we frequently conflate the ideas of leader *emergence* and leader *effectiveness*.

While emergence describes how influential and "leaderlike" someone seems to be, effectiveness is the extent to which that person can in fact do the thing that is leadership.[5,6] The distinction is important because the traits and behaviors that cause us to perceive someone as leaderlike may not be the same traits and behaviors that truly enable someone to gain commitment from a given group and guide them toward achieving a common goal.

Implicit theories, explicit consequences

The questions you ask yourself about whether you can lead are influenced by your environment. With a certain group of people, in a certain kind of organization, amidst a certain type of culture, you may view yourself as more or less capable of leading based on what seems to make leaders successful around you.

For example, you may not be comfortable asserting yourself, and yet you believe and observe in your environment that "leaders are assertive." How then do you square yourself as a leader? Do you decide you can't do it? Do you push yourself to behave more forcefully? You can follow this same line of logic for any characteristic you observe or imagine as part of your implicit theory of leadership.

There's often a gap between how you think about yourself and how you perceive the demands of your position. This is partly why taking on a new role can cause distress. And the distress can intensify if the role you're taking on retains the imprint of its prior inhabitant. Replacing a founder, turning a team around, maintaining a certain growth trajectory; each of these scenarios creates preconceived notions in our minds that can cause us to question whether and how we fit the leadership mold.

What's useful about tuning into your own implicit theory is that you can start understanding your expectations about leadership more clearly and you can start to question whether those expectations serve you. What information is shaping how you define leadership for yourself? What are you reading? What are you observing? What ideas continue to resonate with you about people who are "doing it right"? What leaders do you admire (and what about them do you admire)? In what ways do you find yourself living into your own prototype of leadership (or not)?

The subjunctive ought
These types of influences can be a hard thing to recognize at times, but a good place to start is to try to catch yourself applying your implicit theory to your present circumstances. What do you imagine or wish it were possible for you to do today? When do you think to yourself, "I *should* be doing XYZ," or "I *should* be leading in XYZ way?" What type of action is "the should" suggesting?

The word "should" indicates a certain obligation or sense of correctness, usually in a critical way. So, when *should* starts steering your thinking, you're assuming that there is a correct way to do things, that you have a duty to do things in a certain way, and that doing them differently is representative of some sort of inadequacy or less than desirable action on your part. "I should assert myself more as a leader." "I should be better at giving feedback; once I get better at it, I'll do it more consistently." "If only I could lead more decisively, then I would succeed in this circumstance." Floating off into our fond subjunctives ("I *should...*," "If only I *could...*") is a kind of mental illusion that causes us to ransom our current capability to some future condition.

I think we create this subjunctive ought, these imagined conditions of obligation, because of how we observe leadership in the world around us. The media depicts and describes it in various forms, we hear about it when we listen to podcasts and read books and articles about people in businesses and schools and nonprofits and academia accomplishing great things. There are tens of thousands of books about leaders and leadership out there, many written by or about famous executives or politicians, very accomplished people, all with thrilling tales about what made them successful. We prize these stories of excellence and outsize performance. They're inspiring, sure; but are they useful? Are we able to take the stories of these notable accomplishments and apply them in our everyday lives?

THE EVENT, THE ENDEAVOR, AND THE EVERYDAY

I find that I often play a trick on myself when I think about leadership. I can be enamored with it, I admire it, I hope in it, I count on it. And yet, by pushing it off into the realm of observation and admiration, I limit my day-to-day access to this way of being with other people. Because I don't consistently think about leadership as simply a form of behavior, I let it take on all sorts of shapes and meanings in my mind that make it less useful, less flexible, and less accessible in the here and now.

To challenge my admiration, I've started thinking about leadership as something that can be examined at different levels. Typically, levels of analysis would refer to the individual, group, and organizational level.[7] In this case, I'm referring to when and how we perceive leadership occurring in the culture, levels that I refer to as the event, the endeavor, and the everyday.

The event

The news tends to portray leadership as events that occur with someone at the center. This is the perception of leadership as something that emerges, something that materializes when the atypical happens. We see people step up in these circumstances and say just the right thing, or do something courageous and we say, "that's leadership."

This is the man who, by some instinct or training, gets out in a boat in a 100-year storm and motors house to house, pulling the elderly, trapped, and otherwise infirm into the hull and ferries them to safety. Who continues going out in the flood to find others until he has rescued so many people and become so knowledgeable about how to navigate the streets safely, that he begins helping to direct search-and-rescue missions for the National Guard.[8]

Without a doubt, these are moments of great leadership, but if we view these sorts of acts as indicative of what leadership is, it makes it seem uncommon and foreign. It raises the question, "Could I, or would I, do the same thing in the same circumstances?" Being able to stand up and act – to help, to enliven, to comfort – is a good thing, but this is also a classic example of primarily viewing leadership through the lens of emergence rather than effectiveness. The problem with this perception is that it makes leadership seem like something that happens only in certain circumstances, something that requires crisis, and the more consequential the crisis, the more consequential the leader.

The endeavor

Meanwhile books, articles, and podcasts tend to present leadership as an endeavor, an undertaking in which a bold someone accomplishes something spectacular or unexpected. We see the individual striving in a single-minded way to achieve against the odds, and we call it leadership.

One of my favorite podcasts is *How I Built This* with Guy Raz. It's "a show about innovators, entrepreneurs, idealists, and the stories behind the movements they built." What I like about it is that in many ways, it is the same story told over and over. When I listen to it, I always know what I'm going to get: An intrepid person has an idea, gathers the resources needed (both human and financial) to make that idea a reality, and then persists in it until their vision makes them rich or famous (or, ideally, both).

It is the entrepreneur with a thousand faces. It is the story of the boy who tells his dad he wants to build cars as a kid, and who then aligns everything in his life to support the patient and diligent march toward that idea. From tinkering with cars growing up, to selecting MIT over Stanford's mechanical engineering PhD program because he believed it would better position him to raise money as the founder of an electric vehicle company. From designing a new truck from scratch, to having the vision and the will to work at building it for 12 years before the first one rolled off the production line available for sale.[9]

This is the perception of leadership as pursuit, as the unrelenting drive for success in some venture. It is leadership as entrepreneurial spirit. Now, as I said, I enjoy these stories. They kindle my curiosity, help me to believe that anything is possible, and make me feel engaged in the world in a new way. But that feeling has a short shelf-life and is often followed by a crash back into the questions of my daily existence. Can I lead if I'm not engaged in an equally bold venture? And as interesting as it is to hear about all the twists and turns on the path to success, experiencing those twists and turns as they happen is an entirely different experience than recounting them. What if I don't have the comfort of hindsight? What if I only have the stuff of the present to work with?

How do we classify the minute-to-minute decisions that were made throughout the course of the endeavor; the daily struggles and challenges that were endured; the hard conversations that are always hard, that never get easier no matter how many times you have to have them; the encouragements that helped others to believe that something great was possible? This is all to say, what do we make of the everyday actions and decisions that accumulate over time to enable such endeavors to occur?

The everyday

Without the context of an endeavor or the focal point of an event or crisis, what is left of leadership?

Amid the events and endeavors that we use to describe and valorize acts of leadership, everyday behavior is the connective tissue that allows leadership to happen. The everyday is the most common, the most frequently observed. The most control we have over our thoughts and actions is in the everyday, the here and now, in the very moment. This is why it is so important to consider and understand.

When you zoom all the way in to the day-to-day, past the reams of research, the lists of traits, the expert theories, and the broad pronouncements of founders and CEOs, when you strip away the other psychological concepts that get entangled with leadership – power, authority, boldness, status, success, wisdom, money, charisma, etc. – when you actually encounter someone leading, what is it that you are seeing?

Perhaps it's a café owner who takes the time each morning to check in with each staff member, asking about their well-being, and offering support for their personal and professional growth. Through these conversations, the owner recognizes that her café is a unique environment for working university students, providing the flexibility needed to tend to coursework and the conditions for her young employees to start developing management skills. Over time, she forms partnerships with local universities and businesses, which creates a pipeline for the talent that she needs to run her café and a launching point for new professional opportunities for her "alumni."

You see a person standing in a conference room facilitating a team meeting. A manager who, when conflict arises on their team about how to get a project unstuck, doesn't dictate a solution but facilitates a conversation where each team member can voice their concerns and contribute ideas. And through this conversation, helps the team develop a hybrid approach that combines the best ideas of its members and brings the team closer together in the process.

Maybe it's a person driving their car to work each day by a local park that has fallen into disrepair and disuse, imagining what it would be like to see the park revitalized. But instead of waiting for someone else to work on it, they start sharing their ideas, organizing community meetings to discuss how the park could be brought back to life. They listen to their neighbors and develop a shared vision for the space that they take to the city council. Then, with the support of the community, they wind up organizing a volunteer initiative to help clean up, renovate, and reinvigorate the park.

When you encounter someone leading, odds are you don't see them engaged in grand gestures, what you see are the commonplace, habitual, ordinary interactions with other people that enable and shape the circumstances we call leadership. It is thinking, making decisions, and communicating. Leadership is, at its most fundamental level, just humans in relationship; everything else is storytelling.

Key questions and takeaways

1. **What are your preconceived notions about leadership? How do those notions inform your beliefs about your own ability to lead?**
   a. Our implicit theories of leadership, shaped by cultural, social, and personal experiences, heavily influence how we perceive leaders and leadership effectiveness. Recognizing and examining these preconceived notions can help you understand and challenge your own limiting beliefs about what it takes to lead.

(Continued)

2. **What role do everyday interactions and behaviors play in your perception of leadership?**
   a. Leadership is not solely the result of grand gestures or moments of crisis or achievement but is deeply rooted in everyday actions, decisions, and interactions. Recognizing leadership in the mundane creates an access point for you to begin communicating, supporting, and guiding others in daily contexts.
3. **When you think of things you *should* be doing to be a better leader, what comes to your mind? Where do those *shoulds* come from and how relevant are they to your actual day-to-day life?**
   a. Moving beyond idealized narratives and myths of leadership is critical to embracing the reality that leadership is accessible and doable. This involves a shift from viewing leadership as a distant, performative role to recognizing it as a set of tangible actions and decisions that can be practiced and refined over time.

NOTES

1 Spector, Bert Alan. "Carlyle, Freud, and the great man theory more fully considered." *Leadership* 12, no. 2 (2016): 250–260.

2 One Google search just for "leadership vs management Harvard Business Review" produced at least 10 articles with titles like "Managers and Leaders: Are They Different?", "The Best Managers are Leaders – and Vice Versa," "Three Differences Between Managers and Leaders," etc.

3 Epitropaki, Olga, and Robin Martin. "Implicit leadership theories in applied settings: Factor structure, generalizability, and stability over time." *Journal of Applied Psychology* 89, no. 2 (2004): 293.

4 Epitropaki, Olga, and Robin Martin. "From ideal to real: A longitudinal study of the role of implicit leadership theories on leader-member exchanges and employee outcomes." *Journal of Applied Psychology* 90, no. 4 (2005): 660.

5 Judge, Timothy A., Joyce E. Bono, Remus Ilies, and Megan W. Gerhardt. "Personality and leadership: A qualitative and quantitative review." *Journal of Applied Psychology* 87, no. 4 (2002): 765.

6 Yukl, Gary. "Effective leadership behavior: What we know and what questions need more attention." *Academy of Management Perspectives* 26, no. 4 (2012): 66–85.

7 Lowman, R. L. *An introduction to consulting psychology: Working with individuals, groups, and organizations.* American Psychological Association (2016).

8 Mark Guarino, "A Katrina hero: He hopped into a boat and became a one-man rescue squad," *The Washington Post*, August 23, 2015. https://www.washingtonpost.com/national/the-lifesaver-a-man-grabbed-a-boat-and-did-what-he-could/2015/08/23/697d6274-4043-11e5-bfe3-ff1d8549bfd2_story.html

9 Guy Raz, interview with RJ Scaringe, How I Built This with Guy Raz, podcast audio, September 12, 2022, https://wondery.com/shows/how-i-built-this/episode/10386-rivian-rj-scaringe/

CHAPTER 2

What a leader does

Think about the title of this chapter for just a moment. Depending on what you believe about leaders and leadership positions, you might think *a leader does what a leader does*. Which is to say, it's the person or the position that makes the leader; therefore, whatever they do is by default leadership. We're just left to determine whether that leadership is good or bad, effective or otherwise. If that line of thinking has some resonance for you, I want you to loosen your grip on the thought that leadership is something that necessarily occurs because it comes from a certain place or person. If that were true, then the sum total of leadership-development advice would be essentially "you are one or you aren't one," or "if you want to lead, go get a leadership job."

I've always been more interested in the behaviors that we understand as leadership because it takes the idea of leading out of the realm of the abstract and grounds it in the here and now. What is someone in a leadership position *actually doing* during the day? What types of behavior do we observe and register as leading? There is a humanistic angle to the idea, I think, something that acknowledges the soft animal beneath the concept. For example, surveys suggest that CEOs spend upward of 70% of their time in meetings.[1] If that's true, we learn two potentially interesting facts about what a CEO's day might look like – that meetings dominate their schedule, sure, but also that much of what they're doing is sitting (presumably) and talking to other people.

This is leadership plucked out of the clouds and plopped into the realm of our common humanity. At this level, everyone has access to it. This is the view of leadership as an embodied task, as something that occurs at the level of the

DOI: 10.4324/9781032616193-3

human being thinking, feeling, and behaving. This is a perspective that asks, if I filmed this "leadership" happening, what would I hear? What would I see? What would I think or feel?

If I filmed the CEO sitting and talking to other people, would we necessarily call it leadership? It certainly could be, but if it is, what is it that pushes it beyond just a normal conversation?

EVERYDAY LEADERSHIP

At the everyday level, in the here-and-now, leadership consists of three fundamental elements: anticipation, participation, and cooperation. This is not *the three things that all great leaders do*. This is not a recipe for leadership but points to the principles behind what leadership accomplishes. Each element is a building block, a necessary but not sufficient component. At some point, in some form, all three elements must be present for leadership to occur.

Anticipation

Leadership starts as a thought. When we talk about leaders as people who create a vision that inspires others, or who help provide direction for a team, what we are talking about is their ability to think about the future and communicate that thinking to others. For example, you're reading this book now, but what will you do after you set it down? What do you expect to do tomorrow, or later this week? And how would you explain it to someone else?

What does this look like in action? The owner of a new sandwich shop considers the impact on her business due to pandemic restrictions and reimagines how she might get her products into her customers' hands. Instead of just preparing for a downturn, she stands up an e-commerce store to enable online ordering, buys a remote point-of-sale system to facilitate pick-up orders, and hires a driver to run deliveries throughout the neighborhood. This quick thinking not only allows her business to continue operating but enables her to expand and hire other people. By the time the restrictions ease, she has built up a following in her city and the business continues to flourish.

This is anticipation. In a sense, it is simply thinking about things; but when it comes to leadership, it is thinking about what currently is, and what could be. Anticipation is an act of the imagination. It is the mind's ability to wonder, hope, forecast, expect, and predict. It is the transcendent element of leadership, the art of possibility. But anticipation isn't enough; to lead we must act on what we anticipate.

Participation

At the simplest level, a participant is someone who takes part in something, they get involved, they contribute, they engage. Leadership does not occur if ideas remain ideas. Participation is our ability to make decisions and act in order to bring our ideas into being. Whether that's saying them out loud, writing them down, designing, building, or creating in some way, our ideas must begin to take some physical form in the world to create the opportunity for leadership to occur. The participant keeps working on the idea, pushing it forward, trying to make it real. There is a posture here of leaning in that acknowledges that nothing happens with our ideas if we don't act on them in some way.

A fun example of participation is the technology product manager whose favorite sport is alpine skiing, but who is continually baffled by how uncomfortable ski boots are and the lack of innovation in the industry to address such a basic issue. There must, he imagines, with all the advances in 3D printing and customization technology, be some way of making boots that perform equally well and are actually comfortable to wear. But beyond just imagining the possibility, he digs into the question. He asks other skiers what their least favorite part of skiing is (it's always the boots...), he tinkers with design software that allows him to take a scan of his foot and translate it into a CAD file, and he starts researching materials that he might be able to use to start 3D printing custom ski boot liners. Before long, he has a company, is sharing the idea with other leaders in the sporting goods industry, and building the support he needs to turn this idea into a reality.

Anticipation without participation is purely imaginative, it is daydreaming. Anticipation *with* participation sounds like this, "Hey, I've been thinking about...," "Have you ever wondered why...," "What if we could...," or "Let me show you this idea I'm working on." And as you may surmise based on statements like these, we must also get other people involved.

Cooperation

Leadership only occurs when people work together, when they cooperate to some extent to achieve a common goal. Cooperation is our ability to bring others in, to communicate ideas in such a way that gets people interested, engaged, and involved. That is, it gets others to participate, to work toward the same end with similar expectations and hopes.

Say a filmmaker has an idea for a documentary. A vision for how its style could communicate a message of compassion while telling the story of a group of people in a new and compelling way. This idea takes root, and she begins to act. She seeks out stakeholders who have insight into this group of people to learn more. She spends time watching other films. She reads books and articles that have been written on the same issues. Then she starts telling people about her idea, bringing others into the vision she has. Making a documentary is the type of undertaking that demands a team of people work together for an idea to become a reality. She needs a producer to manage the business of the film, a cinematographer to capture the footage, an editor to edit the tape, and executive producers to help raise money and awareness. And all the while she must find film subjects, develop close working relationships with them and her teams, and hold that vision in mind while navigating the high-highs and low-lows of the creative process.

To be sure, great things may be possible without cooperation, but to align people and resources toward the same vision, to accomplish the types of things that an individual alone cannot accomplish, to do the things that leadership does, cooperation is a necessary component.

I may enjoy daydreaming about my idea or researching my concept and imagining what the future could look like, but imagining possibilities on their own is not something that we call leadership, especially if that imagining only exists in the confines of my own mind. Because leadership is fundamentally social, it can only emerge when ideas are placed into a social context. They must be said out loud. I must act on my ideas such that they have the possibility of involving other people. The moment other people are interested and involved, leadership starts to occur. Everyday leadership asks you to lean into this reality: to take seriously your ideas and expectations for the future, to articulate your understanding of what is and what could be, and to believe that your effort can bring those two realities together.

It requires you to share your thoughts, to interact with and engage other people to accomplish something greater than you could on your own. It is a willingness to take the first step, and the step after that. And this same thing occurs in both complex and quite simple situations.

Getting into the details
What I like about this way of thinking is that it is small and simple, and it gets down to the granular level of what is happening when someone is leading. They are anticipating, participating, and cooperating with others. And we can test this idea by thinking about how it applies to different scales of leadership because at the everyday level, the same components of leadership are always at work.

At the larger scale, say I'm considering how traffic might be rerouted through the city I live in to reduce congestion and increase economic development. The highway runs directly through a key downtown area which creates a number of issues, such as dividing communities, hindering urban development, and promoting car dependency. But I think rerouting the highway, though costly, could increase opportunities for pedestrian mobility and alternative transportation, create more green space and reduce pollution, and generally bring about urban revitalization to the downtown area.

At the smaller scale, say I'm considering how I might best shape the environment into which my kids arrive home from school. With young kids, the end of the day often feels hectic. The kids come home tired and hungry, and it's often a slog to get them to focus on eating dinner and then moving through a bedtime routine in any kind of straightforward way. But I think there are small changes I can make that will help set the tone for the kind of evening we would like to have and create more opportunities for connection and rejuvenation.

In the case of my home life, I simply imagine our evening as a family going a certain way. Achieving this outcome may involve incredibly mundane tasks like turning on the outdoor lights, turning on music, tidying up a bit, having dinner prepared, and having an activity to invite the kids into to channel their energy. Simple actions that create the opportunity for my family to follow my lead, as it were, to be invited into the idea of us spending time together in a certain way rather than just trudging our way toward one more bedtime.

In the case of rerouting traffic, there will be many more tasks required, some of which will undoubtedly be more complicated, the resources dramatically more intensive, the communication more complex, and the stakeholders potentially less receptive, but the essential nature of what's occurring is still anticipation, participation, and cooperation.

In each case, I am considering what is happening and how things could go if I act in certain ways, and furthermore, how my actions might shape other people's perceptions, expectations, and experiences going forward. In both circumstances, I am pursuing my ideas and drawing others into my understanding and perception of things to help achieve an outcome that I imagine is possible.

We do this sort of thinking all day long in every type of circumstance. It's as if the possibility of leading is ever present, we have only to recognize that possibility and give it a try.

If you are learning how to lead, evolving the way you lead, or simply confronting the ongoing challenge of leadership at a new level, this framework is useful because it grounds the task of leading at the level of everyday thinking and action, where it is immediately accessible to you. This is the level of change, the level at which you can begin to alter the way you lead.

EVERYDAY LEADERSHIP BEHAVIOR

Anticipation, participation, and cooperation have become my shorthand for thinking about leadership after years of research, observation, and practice as a leadership coach. It's a model that I hold in my mind as I work through problems with people, help them think about how they might adapt, try new things, and how they might approach the work of leadership in new and interesting ways. To get the most out of this model though, I think it's useful to know where it came from.

A bit of background
When I began my graduate work in consulting psychology, I was most focused on values, interests, and personality. I liked learning about these trait-based constructs because they tend to be consistent across a lifespan and knowing about them can help inform key decisions about work.[2,3] I was intrigued by the many relationships these types of traits share with leadership outcomes, but I quickly encountered a limitation of this research when it came to working with people in the lived reality of their jobs.

Knowing which traits predict which outcomes makes for interesting and useful facts in some circumstances, but also creates a sort of fatalistic paradigm at the individual level. If a trait like extroversion predicts some amount of leadership effectiveness, that fact alone doesn't help an introverted person improve their work as a leader.

So, I gravitated toward leader *behavior* in my research because it seemed to me that behavior was an access point to helping people. For example, when it came to leadership effectiveness, did something like communication skill mitigate the benefit that personality traits may afford?[4] After all, communication skills can be learned, practiced, and improved.

In my doctoral research, I studied whether different types of behavior made people more effective as leaders as their management level increased.[5] I was curious about how the expression of leadership evolved as the context in which it was being practiced evolved. For example, how does leadership change as you move up in a hierarchy, say from managing individual contributors to managing managers? In what ways does your leadership practice need to change to be effective? To answer that question in a useful way, I needed a systematic way of thinking about different types of leadership behavior.

Enter the Ohio State Leadership Studies. This post-WWII research program was run by people from various disciplines (e.g., psychology, sociology, economics) who wanted to better understand the patterns of activity that shaped how leaders spent their time on a daily basis.[6] They focused on behavior because they believed behavior provided a lens into leadership that would be relevant across different domains such as business, education, and government.[7]

Their findings had an intuitive appeal, that a leader's behavior basically factored into two categories, showing "consideration" for others and "initiating structure."[8] Essentially, their work showed that leaders spend their time helping groups navigate changing circumstances by doing things like building relationships, supporting teams, assigning tasks, and making decisions.

Over time, classifications of leader behavior have expanded to include other concepts like ethical behavior, abusive behavior, passive behavior, etc.[9] But the most ubiquitous categories, the ones that continually pop up in over half a century of research on the subject, are those we now think of as relationship-, task-, and change-oriented behavior.[10]

Relationship-oriented behavior

Relationship-oriented leader behaviors focus on establishing, maintaining, and improving interpersonal relationships. These are the things you do to develop trust on teams and to encourage people to work together toward common goals. These behaviors tend to be represented in leadership competency models under titles like collaboration and influence, coaching and developing others, active listening, managing conflict, and team building.

The basic unit of relationship-oriented behavior is the one-on-one meeting. It is sitting down with someone over whom you have some responsibility and making time to be present and listen. The leader who is highly focused on relationship-oriented behavior makes these kinds of interactions a priority. That means not always rescheduling the one-on-one when a client wants to meet at the same time, not overscheduling so that it feels like these meetings are squeezed in between the "truly important" ones, and not waiting until the very last minute in the day so that you're distracted and rushed and thinking about getting out the door. It means attending to the relationship.

At a slightly larger scale, I think of the CEO who would host lunches with employees from across his company.[11] It was not about going to a white tablecloth restaurant to make an impression, it was about communicating with people in his organization more intentionally. He kept the groups small, only inviting three other people each time to ensure the conversation could be intimate and everyone had the chance to participate. And he would invite team members with enough lead time to be able to explain the purpose of the meal, which was to create an opportunity for them to spend time with the head of their organization and develop a relationship with him, and for them to be able to discuss or ask questions about anything related to the company in a candid, confidential setting.

At the everyday level, relationship-oriented behavior is how we get along with others and help others get along. It is tending to the relationships around you to encourage cooperation.

Simple things like asking other people questions, listening to their answers, expressing warmth and appreciation for what they do, being consistent in order to build trust, demonstrating some amount of vulnerability and mutual respect, and showing empathy and support. You can think of relationship-oriented behaviors as those things you do to invest in people, keep the group together, motivated, and energized in the work.

Task-oriented behavior

Task-oriented leader behaviors orient people toward the accomplishment of goals. These are the things we do to achieve our collective objectives by applying expertise, being organized, communicating in a direct manner, monitoring performance, and pushing to deliver outcomes. These are the behaviors leadership competency models might refer to as driving results, setting goals, delegating, holding others accountable, and demonstrating technical/business acumen.

The project leader at a growing software company exemplifies task-oriented leadership behavior through her approach to weekly planning. Every Monday morning, she gathers the team for a brief meeting to set the focus for the week. She briefly reviews achievements from the prior week and highlights things that can be improved, then she outlines the key milestones to be achieved and reiterates priorities based on the project's timeline. She assigns specific tasks to specific team members, ensuring that each person understands their responsibilities and deadlines, and then makes herself available for any questions or updates her team may have. This simple practice helps to keep the team organized, aligned, and clear on what needs to get done by when in order to stay on track.

At the everyday level, task-oriented behavior is simply getting things done and making it easier for other people to get things done. It is tending to the undertaking at hand and stimulating participation. It is talking about specific goals and expectations, creating and communicating plans, assigning tasks, making decisions, and giving constructive feedback. I sometimes think of task-oriented behavior as my "desk work," which may also be the case for you, especially if your role trends toward knowledge work. These are the things you do to keep things moving and progressing in a given day.

Change-oriented behavior

Change-oriented leader behaviors are those that help people adapt, evolve, and see what could be. Changing environments and circumstances require us to do things like share a vision, clarify a mission, or communicate a strategy. Enabling innovation, guiding others through organizational transformation, fostering interaction among different groups of people, and helping people stay responsive to new challenges and opportunities are all change-oriented behaviors. These are complex behaviors, ones you might find in leadership competency models under titles such as strategic thinking, transformational leadership, driving change, and vision casting.

Now I admit, when talking about change-oriented behavior, I am wary of the word "vision." It's not a bad word necessarily, but it can be a bit grandiose – *Casting a Vision* – and thereby misleading in the context of everyday life. Better to think of tuning into your expectations and hopes, the ideas you wonder and daydream about. To the extent you can paint a picture of these things for others and get them interested and engaged, that's change-oriented leadership behavior.

The aim is to help other people think beyond the present circumstances and understand how to take action to get there. It is tending to your own and others' sense of anticipation, of what could be if we accomplish certain things or do things a certain way. That may simply mean taking time to think and make connections on your own, it may mean communicating a strategy with an organization, talking with other people about their hopes and desires for the future, or helping them find or articulate the meaning in what they're doing.

The program coordinator at my graduate school had a notable impact on me in this way. During my first semester of graduate school, I found myself sitting in her office with some frequency asking for guidance. She helped me get a lay of the land, make sense of the various requirements I would need to fulfill, and start to understand which professors might be best to work with. In the process of advising me on these school-related issues though, she also asked me about my career goals. What did I hope to accomplish in graduate school? Why did I want a doctorate? What did I think a doctorate would do for me?

Her coaching was instrumental in shaping my perspective on my degree. I went to school thinking a PhD was an end in itself, that the degree was the point, but these conversations helped me start to understand it as simply an access point into the type of work I wanted to do. Because of her insight and influence, I became far more pragmatic in how I viewed my schoolwork. I started thinking much farther ahead than I would have otherwise, better navigating the timing of different course offerings. I was able to avoid a few pitfalls I may have stepped into on my own, and with her help, I wound up finishing the program a full year faster than I would have otherwise.

PRINCIPLES, NOT RECIPES

Let's take a step back. We've covered a lot of ground in this chapter, from the essential activity that is leadership (anticipation, participation, and cooperation) to the types of behavior that make up these activities (relationship, task, and change). This is the point in this book where it would be easy to slip into pure advice mode. To say that there *is* a secret formula, that all great leaders do these few specific things, and that if you just follow my simple three-step process in *this exact way*, you can achieve leadership greatness. Here's the thing, that's just not true.[12]

Your leadership needs to be responsive to your environment, which is to say, it must serve the people it is intended to impact. Inevitably that will require different iterations, gradations, and manifestations of leader behavior to be effective. Think about how different cooperation (relationship-oriented behavior) might look in the military compared to a startup, or in a manufacturing company compared to a law firm. Think about how different the manifestations of change-oriented leadership behavior (anticipation) could be in a university setting; from a one-on-one conversation between a student and program coordinator to a president helping raise funds to establish a new academic institute aimed at meeting a societal need.[13]

These categories of behavior can help describe the essential elements at play, but because the context of leadership is so critical to its effectiveness, you will need to learn, and in some ways decide, how each element applies to your own unique circumstances.

Key questions and takeaways

1. **At a fundamental level, what do you think about doing when you think about leading other people?**
   a. Leadership is not confined to titles or positions but is an everyday practice. This perspective simplifies the act of leading, making it accessible and achievable for anyone, regardless of their role in an organization.
2. **What are the essential elements of leadership, and how do they manifest in daily activities?**
   a. The core of leadership lies in three elements: anticipating future needs and possibilities, participating actively in the realization of these ideas, and cooperating with others to achieve common goals. These elements serve as the building blocks of everyday leadership. Recognizing and developing these aspects of your behavior can enhance your ability to lead effectively in the here-and-now.
3. **How adaptable and responsive is your approach to leading to your environment?**
   a. Effective leadership is not about following a fixed set of rules but adapting to the unique demands of each situation. Leaders need to be attentive and responsive to the specific needs of their organization, their team, and the people around them.

NOTES

1 Porter, Michael, and Nohria, Nitin. "What do CEOs actually do?" *Harvard Business Review*, July-August (2018).
2 Roberts, Brent W., and Hee J. Yoon. "Personality psychology." *Annual Review of Psychology* 73 (2022): 489–516.
3 Rounds, James, and Rong Su. "The nature and power of interests." *Current Directions in Psychological Science* 23, no. 2 (2014): 98–103.
4 I took up this specific question for my master's thesis and found that generally the higher the communication skill rating, the higher the job performance rating, regardless of personality trait level across each of the Big Five personality traits. So, yes it does.
5 If you dare…Blankenship, J. R. *Self-other agreement and leader effectiveness: Examining differences across leader behaviors and managerial levels.* California School of Professional Psychology (2016).
6 Shartle, Carroll L. "Early years of the Ohio State University leadership studies." *Journal of Management* 5, no. 2 (1979): 127–134.
7 Schriesheim, Chester A., and Barbara J. Bird. "Contributions of the Ohio state studies to the field of leadership." *Journal of Management* 5, no. 2 (1979): 135–145.
8 Fleishman, Edwin A. "The description of supervisory behavior." *Journal of Applied Psychology* 37, no. 1 (1953): 181–210.
9 Kelemen, Thomas K., Samuel H. Matthews, and Kimberley Breevaart. "Leading day-to-day: A review of the daily causes and consequences of leadership behaviors." *The Leadership Quarterly* 31, no. 1 (2020): 101344.
10 Derue, D. Scott, Jennifer D. Nahrgang, Ned ED Wellman, and Stephen E. Humphrey. "Trait and behavioral theories of leadership: An integration and meta-analytic test of their relative validity." *Personnel Psychology* 64, no. 1 (2011): p. 15
11 Gray, Dave. "Communication Lunches," *Stoneybrook Insights* (blog). March 24, 2024. https://mailchi.mp/stoneybrookventures/vol3-17748783?e=f3a98e2568
12 Haslam, S. Alexander, Mats Alvesson, and Stephen D. Reicher. "Zombie leadership: Dead ideas that still walk among us." *The Leadership Quarterly* 35, no. 3 (2024): 101770.
13 Newman, Caroline. "Strengthening American democracy: The University of Virginia's new Karsh Institute of Democracy embraces higher education's critical role in the country's future." *Inside Higher Ed.* https://narratives.insidehighered.com/strengthening-american-democracy/index.html

CHAPTER 3

How the task of leadership evolves

Now that you have a firm understanding of the key elements of leadership and leadership behavior, it's time to consider how leadership behavior evolves. Alas, the ways in which you lead will need to change over time because things are always changing. The composition of your role may change, the context around your role may change, your strategy may change; the people you work with, the place you work, to say nothing of the environment in which your team or organization operates; all will change. Unfortunately, your leadership behavior will need to continually adapt to its environment, regardless of how much leadership know-how, experience, and skill you may have built up.

Consider how the leadership task of a startup founder changes as a company scales. Initially, the founder will be involved in every aspect of the business. From the abstract – imagining and communicating their idea to others – to the concrete – setting up a legal entity, opening a bank account, obtaining any other foundational resources needed to make their product. They'll know every detail of the business, and the leadership task will primarily involve getting others to see what they see, believe what they believe is possible, and join them in making it a reality.

Say they succeed at this stage, develop a useful product, bring together a small team, and find a market for it. The leadership imperative then shifts to scaling the business, which usually means hiring more people. The team starts growing, that means there are more people around to take on the workload, but the increased headcount also means that new management processes and systems may now be required. Instead of focusing on the day-to-day operations, the founder is now focused on building out and developing their team so they can continue to scale. Perhaps they're recruiting people with more experience and know-how and will need to prioritize communicating how they envision the company continuing to grow, why their strategy makes them competitive, and what exit opportunities may exist for the business. Effectively, while succeeding in building a company, the nature of the leadership task changed around them.

Fortunately, there are some systematic ways in which the work of leadership evolves, and these same patterns occur in organizations of all sizes as people move around, and teams form and transform. There are a few frameworks that can help you evaluate circumstances and gain insight into how you may need to adjust your approach as the scope and scale of your leadership context change. This may involve thinking differently about the time horizon of your role, the balance between control and influence, and the effect of uncertainty on the practice of leadership.

THE TIME HORIZON OF YOUR ROLE

A job's time horizon is not something we typically think about in everyday life. What I mean by time horizon is basically how much time you need to complete a given task effectively.[1] For some tasks, the horizon may be quite short, taking only a bit of time, or a day or a week to complete. For others, the time horizon may extend out to months or years. In some industries, the strategic time horizon occurs at the level of decades and even centuries (think energy and utilities, insurance, space exploration, etc.).

Practically speaking, let's take the simple example of a coffee shop to consider how a time horizon may change. At the entry level, you will likely be taking orders from customers and making drinks. Most of the tasks that constitute your role may take only a few moments to complete and don't tend to string together day-to-day. You can successfully complete each shift by taking orders and pouring cups.

Now say you get promoted to store manager, a role that involves longer term tasks like organizing shifts, hiring, inventory management, and planning for holidays. The time horizon of your role has expanded from one day to, say, six months. To successfully complete the tasks of your role, you're thinking weeks and months ahead so that you can ensure the right resources are in place for the store to operate and meet customer needs on an ongoing basis.

Now, let's zoom out. Say you had some ideas about how to build a coffee shop brand or how to roast beans in a certain way, and you enjoyed managing the coffee shop so much that you started your own company. Your role may now involve tasks that operate on the scale of a year or more. For example, you'll need to manage things like securing a lease, hiring and staffing, and buying insurance. Perhaps you'll need to raise money from investors, which will involve not only describing how the coffee shop will work on a functional level, but also why you think it's a good investment over the long term.

As you get rolling though, you find that you're not pleased with the quality of the beans you can source from local suppliers, so you decide to develop your own supply chain. You start learning how to find and partner with coffee bean farmers in South America. You learn more about how coffee beans grow and the terroir that creates the exact quality and taste that you're trying to produce in your shop back in your hometown. Your brand comes to represent not only high-quality coffee but also sustainable and ethical farming practices. Before you know it, you've created a job with a time horizon that operates on the scale of years, perhaps even a decade or more.

The same kind of evolution happens in all different kinds of work as the scale of leadership increases. This can inform how you think about effective leadership because if you're trying to accomplish a longer term leadership task in a shorter term way (or vice versa), you will find yourself frustrated, ineffective, confused, or all the above. For example, building an effective team frequently requires some amount of time; relationships need to form, trust needs to build. Neglecting this *affective* part of team development or trying to force this process to happen too quickly can have the opposite effect on effectiveness.[2] Considering the time horizon of your role is critical also because a longer horizon tends to mean managing more complexity, thinking farther out into the future, and operating at a higher level. In practice, this usually means an increasing focus on influence.

THE BALANCE BETWEEN CONTROL AND INFLUENCE

As the scale of your leadership increases, you tend to have less direct control over tasks and how they get completed. This is a bit odd because the same increase in scale tends also to bring more power and discretion to decide what tasks (or goals, or strategies) should be pursued. But the higher you get in a hierarchy, the less tangible impact you tend to have on the actual doing of the thing.

Part of the reason this happens is the increasing horizon of your work, which means that the tasks that you're working on necessarily require more time to bring to fruition. The other reason this happens is that the connection between cause and effect in your work becomes more ambiguous. As your role gets more complex, you must rely more on others to get things done. Accordingly, as you move up in a hierarchy, the more likely it is that the people you rely on are also relying on others to get things done. There is a sort of cascading effect involved as the leadership-influence network expands.

Take a very practical example of a task-oriented leader behavior like articulating an organizational goal. On the smaller scale that may be as simple as assembling your team and having a conversation about when a project needs to be completed. On a larger scale, that may involve assembling your team and creating a communication strategy, planning when and how others will communicate with their teams, and how those messages will roll out at different organizational levels on a schedule over the course of weeks or months. Instead of making sure a few people know what you're talking about, you now must ensure that your organization is aligned with the overarching goal, that the members of your team know how their goals fit into the overarching goal, and that they can communicate the same to the people reporting into them, etc.

This is why influence becomes so much more important at higher levels, and why the adaptation to different levels of leadership can be so challenging; the nature of what it means and feels like to be productive changes. When you start working, you're typically focused on yourself, what you can do and what you need to accomplish to be successful. Leading requires taking other people into account.

On a smaller scale, that may only involve thinking about, managing, and tending to a few other people, while on a larger scale, it could be hundreds or thousands. For example, the head of an organization may be most productive when simply providing guidance and approval for different courses of action rather than doing things that make them feel productive. Instead of doing the thing and seeing it get done, you shift into asking someone else to do the thing, or asking someone else to make sure others get the thing done. The further you get from the task itself, the more the task of leadership becomes one of relationship management, communication, and influence. What this means at the level of the everyday is that it may not always be possible to look back over the events of a day and know exactly what was accomplished or what kind of progress was made.

THE EFFECT OF UNCERTAINTY

Baked into all this talk about how the task of leadership changes is the fact of change itself. Because change is a part of what leading is addressing for a group of people, there is a kernel of uncertainty at the core of what it means to lead.

Let me tell you something, *many* people struggle to adjust to this uncertainty. They find themselves in a role that requires leading and then, rather than acknowledging and engaging with the ambiguity of it all, they just continue doing whatever it was that got them into the position in the first place. Usually, this amounts to whatever it is that still makes them feel productive; digging into a spreadsheet, writing a contract, visiting customers…insert your own activity here. The reason we do this is because shaping a task can be uncomfortable and intimidating. It's inexact. It's much easier to stick with the things we know how to do, to do the things we're told to do, or wait until we feel the path forward is perfectly clear. But part of the work of leadership is evaluating what's going on around you and making a judgment about what needs to be done in response and how. The nature of the task is to shape the task.

This is what got me so interested in leadership assessment and succession planning in the first place.[3] If part of the job of leading is to shape the job to properly respond to the context, then there is always a piece that is unknowable.

In fact, much of the work I do now is helping people think through these uncertain elements of leadership. Creating space to consider all kinds of ambiguous questions, from "Am I doing this right?" or "Should I hire this person?" to "Who should lead this organization in the future?" and "How do I adapt as my role changes?"

As you may imagine, these conversations tend to be heavily focused on the future. We spend a lot of time talking about what we know now, how the present may shape what's to come, and how to navigate complex decisions with imperfect information.

What's interesting about these kinds of conversations is that they almost exactly describe the conditions of anxiety. Anxiety is "worry, nervousness, or unease, typically about an imminent event or something with an uncertain outcome."[4] That's not to say that the uncertainty of leading is always, or even frequently, characterized by *worry, nervousness, and unease,* but it is quite frequently characterized by *imminent events with uncertain outcomes.* And this, I think, is where some discomfort comes from. When you are leading, it is your job to interact with that uncertainty on behalf of other people.

Adjusting to the task of leading, then, means reconciling yourself to a task that can be innately anxiety producing. That's why it's so important to consider the fundamental nature of leadership and to ground yourself in the behaviors that constitute leading. This becomes the toolkit you can draw from when you look around yourself in a given moment and think, "What might make for effective leadership in a situation like this?" and then giving that a try.

Key questions and takeaways

1. **How would you define the time horizon of your current role? Are you going through a transition where the time horizon is changing?**
   a. Leadership is not static; as organizations grow and change, and as you move up in a hierarchy, the time horizon of your role may change. Being mindful of the time horizon your role is operating on can be a key element in understanding how to be effective.
2. **How do you manage the balance between control and influence?**
   a. Frequently leadership transitions require a reevaluation of how much direct control you have over the outcomes you are aiming to accomplish. Evaluating how much of your role requires influence, and when and how to deploy influence, can be a useful way of adjusting to a changing scope of leadership.
3. **What strategies can you employ to manage the inherent uncertainty in your role?**
   a. Embracing uncertainty and change is a fundamental part of leading. You can help manage this uncertainty by seeking feedback, finding ways to foster flexibility in your approach, and continuously reassessing and aligning your actions with the demands of the environment.

NOTES

1 Jaques, Elliott. "The development of intellectual capability: A discussion of stratified systems theory." *The Journal of Applied Behavioral Science* 22, no. 4 (1986): 361–383.
2 Bernstein, Ethan. "Leadership and teaming." *Harvard Business School* (2013).
3 Blankenship, J. Ross. *Assessing CEOs and senior leaders: A primer for consultants*. American Psychological Association (2022).
4 *New Oxford American Dictionary*. 2nd ed. Edited by Erin McKean (New York: Oxford University Press, 2005), s.v. "anxiety."

CHAPTER 4

Learning how you practice leadership

There is something deeply instinctive about the idea that, at its core, the mechanism of leadership is helping people get along, get things done, and navigate change. In fact, you can likely consider these broad categories of behavior in your own life and already get a sense for what you tend to be best and worst at, what you tend to spend more or less time doing.

In some ways, it's easy to reflect on your own experience and circumstances and develop some understanding. Are you more focused on the people around you or the tasks in front of you? Do you spend more time trying to get the strategy right or ensuring people get their work done? Thinking through what you do with your time, how you embody your leadership work, and, more importantly, how those around you perceive your leadership work, can help you identify where you may be strongest and where you might need development or support. It also gives you an avenue for considering what might be missing from your specific recipe of leadership behavior when you aren't achieving the outcomes you're aiming to achieve.

But self-knowledge can also be quite limited.[1] And to complicate matters further, leadership positions themselves can create a sort of looking-glass effect in which gaining a clear-eyed view of the impact you're having on others becomes a challenge. The people around you may have a vested interest in winning you over, maintaining your favor, or shaping your perceptions, which is to say, they may not provide an accurate reflection.

DOI: 10.4324/9781032616193-5

Taking on the work of leadership is committing to a process of learning; to self-reflection, feedback-seeking (i.e., asking other people what they observe), situational awareness, and something like improvisation. It is finding ways to understand the impact you're having and whether (and how) you might need to adjust and test new ways of behaving in order to be more effective.

LEARNING HOW YOU LEAD

What comes naturally?

A useful first step in learning how you lead is to develop an understanding of your own skills and preferences. One way to think about this is to consider what kinds of leadership behavior tend to give you the most energy. What do you want to spend your time doing on a day-to-day basis? Do you want to sequester yourself and dream up new products, ideas, and solutions? Would you prefer collaborating with other people all day long, building strong relationships and finding ways to create bonds that drive your business forward? Or do you want to dig into the operation and execution of things, checking tasks off your list, reviewing documents, and ensuring others are also on track as well? Do you prefer the role of anticipator, cooperator, or participant?

Your tendencies and capabilities emerge from your natural preferences, early experiences, and how you grow up in your work. For example, say you're naturally organized, you color-code your spreadsheets, and you demonstrated some ability to manage a project and keep people on the same page, it's likely that you got more of that work to do as you came along in your career. There's a sense of attraction, selection, and attrition at play in the way we are drawn to certain types of work, demonstrate or develop some ability, and get more of that work (or wash out).

Dig into these kinds of details about your life. What comes naturally to you? How does it create opportunities and limitations in the way you think about leading others? Developing this kind of insight helps you identify sources of energy that can fuel your most natural leadership posture. This is useful information to consider because we tend to gravitate toward tasks and environments that give us energy and sustain our attention.

What do you do now?

Think about the broad categories of leader behavior discussed in Chapter 2 (task, relationship, and change) and consider how you spend the majority of your time. Break it down to the level of a single day. What is it that you're doing physically? If you took out a piece of paper and divided it into three columns – tasks, relationships, and change – and wrote down all the things you did in a day, categorizing each as best you could, what would you learn about how you spend your time? What would you learn if you looked back over the past week of activity and meetings?

This is where it can also be quite helpful to get other people's input. Ask your boss, your peers, or your team. Ask your board, your investors, or your customers. Ask your spouse or your partner. Ask people who can provide you with believable input about how you spend your time, what you do that makes you more effective, and what you do that gets in your way.

Now, this is sometimes easier said than done. As I mentioned previously, leadership positions themselves can shape reality around you such that it can be hard to get an honest read on the impact of your behavior at times. Also, it can just be exceedingly uncomfortable to get candid feedback. That's why it can be useful to have a trusted third party gather feedback on your behalf and help you process the information afterward. In any case, the goal here is to develop some perspective on what you do, what works well, and what doesn't.

What does your environment demand?

To be effective, the means of leadership must align with the demands. You may quite accurately understand your motives, behavior, and your impact on others, but if those things are not a match for your environment or the challenge you're facing, it won't amount to much. If what is needed is a clearer direction, working harder may only generate fruitless activity. If what is needed is a stronger team identity and sense of belonging, it may not matter how compelling the vision is.

Consider the leader who has a propensity for taking charge, making decisions, and driving others to get things done. This leadership approach may be effective in turnaround and crisis situations where people need to get aligned quickly, decisions need to be made, and a bias for action can help reduce uncertainty; it may also be destructive in situations that do not demand that kind of leadership (e.g., when innovative thinking is needed).

Thinking about the demands of your environment is essentially a strategic question. It is asking, "what are we trying to accomplish?" continually to evaluate how expectations and effort are lining up with the effect you're having.

What's the hardest part?

Before, I asked the question, "do you prefer the role of anticipator, cooperator, or participant?" Another way to apply that lens to the situation is to consider the most challenging part of the leadership task you're taking on. Are you in an environment where it's genuinely hard to imagine what the team or the organization should be doing to be successful? Is the task itself hard? Is it complicated, or physically demanding, or resource intensive? Is it a challenge to get others engaged in the idea, to see it or want the same thing?

Frequently, the demands of the environment and your natural leadership tendencies align in some way to make certain leadership tasks easy and others more of a challenge. Say you're an exceptional salesperson who gets promoted into the role of sales leader. Overnight, your job becomes management, not sales, your peers become your direct reports, your favorite task – taking clients out for a beer to talk about sports and upcoming orders – is no longer exactly relevant to day-to-day effectiveness in your job. Perhaps you find that the elements of leading that involve participation and cooperation are not so challenging. You enjoy encouraging other salespeople in their work, helping them hone their systems for productivity and holding them accountable to a high standard of performance, but you really struggle with designing a strategy for how to grow the business beyond the existing region. The strategic element is outside your experience and comfort zone, and because it's uncomfortable, you just focus in on what you know how to do well.

What is your natural leadership posture telling you about gaps in your leadership behavior, or the kind of team you need to build? Who could add that strategic element to the team? What kind of support systems could help you be most effective in a given day? Said another way, how do you take this kind of insight and put it into practice?

PRACTICING LEADERSHIP

I like the word practice when talking about leadership. Practice is about moving from knowing to doing. It's about application, tinkering, and testing new ways of working. It implies that effective leadership – doing the thing well – is not something that is attained but pursued. It's not about getting the trophy, it's about the day-in-day-out intention to show up and work on improving.

Unfortunately, I don't know who you are, who you're working with, or what you're trying to accomplish, so I can't provide any specific guidance on what the path of development may look like for you. But "practice" assumes you're learning and trying new things, you're pushing yourself, and you're opting into getting uncomfortable to progress in your craft. To learn how you may need to develop, my encouragement is to get curious, get creative, and get comfortable being uncomfortable.

Get curious

The word *curious* here is doing double work. Of course, I mean that inquisitiveness is an important way of thinking. The desire to know or understand is the mindset that leads to new insight. It is the way of being in the world that opens you up to new ideas and new perspectives about yourself and others.

But I also like the part of curiosity that implies oddness. This is not exactly an encouragement to be strange for the sake of strangeness, but it is an encouragement to recognize that your individual perspective is unique. The key insights that you can provide may come from the ways that you think differently. What are the questions you have that no one is asking? What is obvious to you but doesn't yet seem to be observed or acknowledged by others? Tune into that frequency. Learn how to turn the volume up on these insights and express them to other people when needed.

Get creative

Your understanding of yourself and your circumstances is maturing, you're tuning into your unique perspective on what's happening around you, it's time to try something new. Change the way things have been done, test your assumptions. Delegate something important, try new ways of working with other people.[2] Try a new meeting format, fewer meetings, a new policy, no policies. See how things evolve and what you can try next.

Note: This is not me saying *develop new habits*. New habits may emerge out of trying new behaviors, but this is tinkering and testing. This is upstream of habits. This is pushing back against doing the same thing over and over, relying only on what comes naturally to you and hoping for different results. You're experimenting with new ways of doing things. You're trying to learn what works, looking for inklings of cause and effect between your behavior and how others respond to you, observing the results you get and evaluating how they line up with your expectations.

Get comfortable being uncomfortable

The good news is that you're trying new things, and the bad news is that pushing yourself into new territory rarely feels good. It can make you feel like you don't know what you're doing, like you're under-qualified, like you're an imposter. It takes attention and effort and energy.

Our brains are designed to conserve energy, to do things in the easiest way possible. Learning something new quite literally requires your brain to develop and strengthen new neural connections. That's why it can be uncomfortable and exhausting. It feels bad because it's not easy.

This is useful. Some amount of discomfort can be your signal that you're leaning into your curiosity and trying something new. Use that feeling as a guide. If you're opting into a little discomfort and using it to develop, you may find it can help you learn to become more adaptable and resilient to changing circumstances.

BEING A LEADER

In the opening of this book, I say *who you are is how you lead*. I mean that less as an assertion and more as an observation. That is to say, you're you, and it's you who's doing the leading here, there's no escaping that fact. Your thoughts, your decisions, and your behavior are shaping the way you engage with others.

This is why I think everyone needs to develop their own theory of leadership to some extent. If you have a clear sense of what you value and how your values shape your attention and your behavior, you can start to be more intentional about the choices you make and how those choices serve what you're trying to accomplish. We must each learn for ourselves what is shaping how we prioritize and make decisions, what we focus on, how we relate to others, and how our attention gives form to the outcomes that emerge around us.

Values shape attention

Your values are your beliefs about what's most important in life. They are the priorities that shape how you organize your time, the people you spend time with, the activities you pursue, and the work environments you seek out.

Your values tend to be relatively stable over the course of your lifetime. They solidify, along with personality and interests, in your 20s and only tend to change when you go through major life events (e.g., first job, marriage, birth of a child, mid-life, death of a parent, etc.).[3] There is good psychological footing here for understanding what drives you, what you're drawn to, what you're trying to accomplish in life.

From a leadership standpoint, what interests me about values is that we all seem to want our values to inform how we lead others. I think it serves as an access point to authenticity. If my leading is informed by my principles, it will come from a more reliable and sustainable place. We do this at the organizational level as well. We try to get a clear sense of our collective values, we try to articulate them so they can inform our decisions, and then we paint them on the walls in bright colors to try to reinforce the idea that we share "core values" in the way we work. The idea of prioritizing what's most important makes a lot of intuitive sense when we're talking about groups of people trying to do things together.

Ah, but there's a problem here isn't there? Take a classic example, what if my top value is family, but I attend most to work? Or at the organizational level, what if our top value is safety, but we focus most on profitability? Are we not living by our values in these circumstances, or can our attention tell us something about what we truly value?

I think of this as the difference between what we *value* and what we're *valuing*. It can be a real challenge to live out our values with the same verve that we express them. Sometimes the things we say we value, that we think we value, that we desperately want to value, are not in fact not where our attention rests.

Attention shapes behavior
Your attention is in some ways your most valuable resource. It is how you harness and direct your mental and physical energy toward some end. There is much to be said

about voluntary versus involuntary attention, the difference between directing your attention toward something by choice and it being naturally drawn to (or captured by) something in your surroundings. Indeed, the world we live in now has become a battleground for your attention.[4,5] But here I want to focus on the voluntary kind, how we direct our attention and decide what to focus on.

When I was in graduate school, I had an immense amount of reading to do each day and never enough time. I probably stayed up late six nights a week trying to get it all done. My days had this consistent pattern in which I would read and finish assignments in the morning; go to class in the afternoon where I'd get more reading assigned; come home and eat dinner with my wife; and then as she was headed to bed, I'd go start reading again into the night. It was never a fun moment, but once I had gotten myself to my desk and opened a book, something would happen. I'd get a few sentences in and think *oh yeah, this is really interesting.* The more I attended to it, the more it drew me in. I'd found a topic that gave me energy, that captured my attention, and so I lent more of my attention to it. Over time, this behavior became a doctoral degree in psychology.

I think of this as the tendency for attention to accumulate. A sort of virtuous spiral is sparked by what we view as important, we attend to it, spend time focused on it, our interest in it (or dedication to it) deepens, we attend to it more, view it as more important, etc. In this way, our interests become the things we repeatedly do, which is how our attention shapes our behavior.

Now, this can have positive and negative effects. We can attend to things that can produce the outcomes we're interested in, or we can continually attend to things that don't serve our best interest. Think about how this can play out in a team setting.

Let's revisit the sales team example. Say I take over the lead for a sales team that has demonstrated solid, consistent performance, but I'm focused on growth. New accounts, that's how we make money. So, I tell my team, figure out ways to open new accounts. I start referring to our clients a little bit differently, now I call them customers. Our motto becomes some version of *do whatever it takes to hit the numbers*. When we hit our quarterly targets, I take my team out to the local steakhouse where the mood is high and the tab is open, you want the $150 dry-aged bone-in ribeye? It's all yours. My team is incredibly profitable and outperforms other teams in the organization, even the industry. But then, years into our high performance, it becomes evident that under all the pressure to sell, my team figured out ways to pad their numbers, opening new accounts without consent and pushing products clients didn't need.

In effect, this is what happened at Wells Fargo.[6] Unrealistic goals and intense pressure trained everyone's attention on achieving results at all costs.[7] Over time, that behavior created a pressure cooker culture in which this kind of thing can happen.

Behavior shapes culture

When people cooperate to accomplish a common goal, they naturally gravitate toward ways of cooperating that make them effective.[8] The behavior of the group leader helps shapes group behavior because the members of a group look to the leader to understand how to succeed. In this way, culture is an emergent thing. It is not something you can grab ahold of and change. Culture is more like an ecology, which means the way you alter it is by thinking about the parts of the system and tinkering with them to see how the ecology adapts.

Effectively what you are doing when you are attending to your own behavior is helping to shape the cultural reality around you. If you are in a leadership position, people are observing you. They are taking cues from what you do as an indicator of what is right, good, and effective. This plays out every day in our families, our teams, our organizations, and in our public discourse. What leaders do informs what we view as ok to do.

Ultimately, the work of being a leader means learning the kind of leadership that is natural to you and the ways of interacting with others that give you energy, then understanding how that serves the environment you're in. This doesn't mean you won't have gaps, that you won't need help from others, or that you won't need to learn how to do new things, but it's an important well to tap because this is where leadership behavior is most sustainable over time. It comes from the most natural place within you, which is to say it's the most *you* way that you might go about leading others. What is the way you can lead that is most natural to yourself?

Key questions and takeaways

1. **How do you balance your natural tendencies with the learned behaviors that are necessary for effective leadership?**
   a. Learning to lead requires a balance between what comes naturally to you and skills that need to be developed. Recognizing and developing your natural leadership style, while also learning new behaviors is crucial for guiding others effectively.
2. **How well does your leadership behavior align with the demands of your environment?**
   a. The effectiveness of your leadership is contingent upon how well it meets the needs of your environment. Assessing how your leadership style matches what is needed around you can help ensure you are leading in a way that positively impacts your team or organization.
3. **What strategies can you employ to become more adaptable and open to feedback in your leadership practice?**
   a. Embracing curiosity, creativity, and a willingness to be uncomfortable are key strategies for evolving as a leader. Actively seeking feedback, being open to new ideas, and experimenting with different leadership behaviors can lead to greater *adaptability and effectiveness over time.*

NOTES

1 Wilson, Timothy D., and Elizabeth W. Dunn. "Self-knowledge: Its limits, value, and potential for improvement." *Annual Review Psychology* 55 (2004): 493–518.

2 Gallo, Amy. *Getting along: How to work with anyone (even difficult people)*. Harvard Business Press (2022).

3 Milfont, Taciano L., Petar Milojev, and Chris G. Sibley. "Values stability and change in adulthood: A 3-year longitudinal study of rank-order stability and mean-level differences." *Personality and Social Psychology Bulletin* 42, no. 5 (2016): 572–588.

4 Crawford, Matthew B. *The world beyond your head: On becoming an individual in an age of distraction*. Farrar, Straus and Giroux (2015).

5 Pedersen, Morten Axel, Kristoffer Albris, and Nick Seaver. "The political economy of attention." *Annual Review of Anthropology* 50 (2021): 309–325.

6 Department of Justice. "Wells Fargo Agrees to Pay $3 Billion to Resolve Criminal and Civil Investigations into Sales Practices Involving the Opening of Millions of Accounts without Customer Authorization." February 21, 2020. Office of public affairs website. https://www.justice.gov/opa/pr/wells-fargo-agrees-pay-3-billion-resolve-criminal-and-civil-investigations-sales-practices

7 McLean, Bethany. "How Wells Fargo's Cutthroat Corporate Culture Allegedly Drove Bankers to Fraud," *Vanity Fair*, Summer 2017.

8 Schein, Edgar H., and Peter A. Schein. *Organizational culture and leadership*. 5th ed. Wiley (2016).

CHAPTER 5

What are you trying to accomplish?

In Chapter 4, we come to rest on the idea that to be the most effective leader you can be, you must tap into a way of leading that comes from a natural place within you.

Now, this doesn't mean *only do what comes naturally*. There are things about leading that must be learned. For example, holding people accountable for results is not exactly something that comes naturally, it's the type of thing you can only really learn how to do once you're in the position to do it. This type of behavior may come more naturally to some than others, but what needs to be learned is how *you* can best hold people accountable. There also may be things that come quite naturally to you that are detrimental to your ability to lead effectively. Some people, when they get anxious and stressed, pull away from others and want to be alone to process and problem solve. This is a stress response that may work well in an individual contributor role, but when you're in the position to be leading others, that means you're disappearing right when things are most stressful and they may need you most.

Finding your natural leadership posture is important, not because it solves all your development needs, but because you need access to the motivating core that drives you or draws you toward leadership. You need to be able to answer questions like this: In taking on the responsibility of leading others, what is it that you're after? What are you trying to accomplish?

If you've been paying attention, you know this simple question is woven throughout the content of this book. And yet, it can be a surprisingly challenging question to answer.

DOI: 10.4324/9781032616193-6

Have you thought about it explicitly? It's an important thing to think about because the answer to that question is how you'll tap into the motivation that we're after.

DIGGING INTO THE QUESTION

When I ask this question in a coaching conversation – *what are you trying to accomplish?* – the response I usually hear is something like, "you mean in work, or more generally?" To this I tend to say – *yes*.

I find this response somewhat revealing. People tend to jump right into what they're trying to accomplish at work. "I'm trying to grow the footprint of my business in the state," or "I'm trying to put together a rockstar team that can build and ship this product," or "I'm trying to increase our annual recurring revenue to X amount so I can sell my business for Y." The metrics are clearer in a work context, the logic of the question makes a bit more sense. But more generally? In life? The answers come a bit slower, tend to be a bit vaguer, and generally amount to "I'm not really sure."

What are you trying to accomplish in your life? What is it that you want your life to have been about?

To be fair, this can be a hard question to answer. And, in some ways, the answer may change as you change and as the things around you change. But I like that the question brings into the foreground the unwieldy notion that work and life are some-how distinct or that they exist on different planes of reality; that work and life must be weighed and compared on a balance scale or woven together like a rope. Think of the cliches, "work-life balance," or, as has become more popular in recent years, "work-life integration." This false dichotomy papers over the fact that there is only life, and work is just a part of it.

In his classic article "How Will You Measure Your Life?", renowned Harvard Business School professor Clayton Christensen lays this reality out in a compelling way. He describes seeing the lives of his 1979 HBS classmates unfold,

"I've seen more and more of them come to reunions unhappy, divorced, and alienated from their children. I can guarantee you that not a single one of them graduated with the deliberate strategy of getting divorced and raising children who would become estranged from them. And yet a shocking number of them implemented that strategy."[1]

For better or worse, work is just part of the living that we do. It is a part of the whole. If you are primarily focused on what you're trying to accomplish in your work, that is what you're primarily trying to accomplish in your life. Fundamentally then, questions about your career are questions about your life.

Over the past ten years of coaching leaders, I've had conversations about this kind of thing many times. These are the most interesting conversations about leadership because they point to how intimately intertwined leading is with identity. I've found that these conversations about leadership and identity tend to take on certain shapes.

There are conversations that are straightforward; troubleshooting a problem, providing direct emotional support, or taking a pragmatic look at what to do and/or ways to try to get something done. Then there are conversations that have more of an arc to them; they're a bit more conceptual and involve thinking through broader ideas, planning, goal setting, and considering strategic trade-offs. And there are the holistic conversations; conversations that zoom all the way out to the facts of being human and the limitations that reality imparts on trying to do things in the world, to take on projects, and to relate to people in a meaningful way. These patterns have been so common that I've started arranging them into a kind of coaching model I call "thinking in frames."

THINKING IN FRAMES

Framing describes our ability to imagine different perspectives to help us understand and navigate the world around us.[2] Given the infinite complexity in the world, our ability to simplify things and generate alternatives through framing helps us develop a point-of-view that can provide insight and a foundation for understanding and decision-making.

Framing is everywhere in life and impacts all our decisions. From how we think about risk (e.g., am I avoiding a loss or pursuing a gain?), to how we buy meat at the grocery store (e.g., am I buying "80% lean," or "20% fat"?), to how we think about and present a given subject matter (e.g., in this book, I'm approaching leadership from a psychological, as opposed to, say, a sociological or economic frame).

Thinking in frames, then, is a specific type of framing tool that helps you think through your values, goals, and career decisions to clarify the problems you're trying to solve and ultimately, what you're trying to accomplish. The three frames are the *pragmatic,* the *strategic,* and the *existential.* The aim of this method is to cycle through different questions and perspectives, to consider a goal or a decision within the parameters of each frame, then shift between the frames to bring to the fore how your perspective changes on the issue at hand. I'll take each frame in turn.

The pragmatic frame

The pragmatic is, as the name implies, the most straightforward. It is the frame in which you think through what's immediately relevant and important to a decision. What resources are necessary, and what resources do you have? How much authority, power, or control do you have in the situation or the decision you're facing? At the pragmatic level, you're evaluating the degrees of freedom you have in choosing what to do. What I mean by degrees of freedom is how many pieces of the decision or problem are moveable or changeable? For example, if you have five books that you need to put in order on a shelf, and I tell you that you can put them in any order you want as long as the red book comes first, then you have four degrees of freedom in making the rest of your choices. In this way, the pragmatic frame orients you in the world as it exists today and focuses you in on what's most controllable in the present moment.

A simple example here is making a job change. Say the fixed point is something like "As long as I make X amount of money, I can take any job I want, anywhere I want." Knowing that you need to make a certain amount of money in a job change is useful because it can serve to immediately eliminate any idea or opportunity that doesn't fit that parameter. If an incredibly attractive opportunity comes up in your dream city, but it doesn't align with the pivot point you've established about salary, you can decisively (if not easily) turn it down. It's also useful to think about this explicitly because it raises other relevant questions such as why do you need to make X amount of money? How fixed is that point and what is fixing it? Those are useful questions to ask yourself because you may find you can adjust that point in order to accomplish something different in the future.

The strategic frame

The strategic frame introduces a narrative arc, it invites you to consider what you can do today that will help shape possible outcomes in the future. The strategic frame is when you start looking ahead at where you'd like your work to get you, how you plan and adapt as things change, and what you predict is possible based on choices you make today. If the pragmatic frame is where you have the most control and the most ability to act, the strategic frame encourages you to think about how your decisions and actions in the present may accumulate over time to different types of outcomes. The strategic frame is where you add in the phrase, "in order to," "I'm going to try X in order to do Y." This is where you start to think about the tradeoffs and sacrifices you're willing to make to try to create certain conditions in the future.

Let's stick with our current example about making a certain amount of money in a job change. Thinking through the decision in the pragmatic frame, you think you need to make X amount. But an opportunity comes along that offers X/2. In the pragmatic frame, that's a "no" because it doesn't meet our basic criteria. But what if the job has the possibility of making 2X within two years? This is where being able to shift into a different framing is useful. At the pragmatic level, this opportunity may be irrelevant and not worth pursuing, but at the strategic level, you may start to think about how the opportunity can create new possibilities in your career. Perhaps it's worth taking a pay cut in the short term for the possibility of making more in the future, or moving into a new part of an organization, or a new field entirely. This is the level at which we start to actively consider how fixed those degrees of freedom are. Sometimes it's worth examining them a bit to create space for new possibilities to emerge. And sometimes it's worth considering, or totally reevaluating, what we're making decisions about, or how we're making decisions in the first place.

The existential frame
The existential frame is the broadest possible frame. It is the level at which you are concerned with being a person in the world. The level at which you situate yourself beyond thoughts of tasks or goals, money or titles, or even of work, to consider life itself and the implications that different choices may have on how you think about spending your time on earth. This is where we season our thinking with the existential givens with which we all must grapple – the fact of death and the search for purpose and meaning.[3] This is where we aim to ask the hard to answer questions about life: Where do I come from? Where am I going? What shall I do while I'm here? What's it all about anyway?

Say the pragmatic and strategic frames exist within a container, the existential frame involves picking the container up and looking at its structure, its seams, and questioning how the whole thing is put together. It is recognizing that this is the container you've built, through decisions you've made, interests you've pursued, opportunities you've seized, and asking the question, "what do I do with this container?"

In our example about making a career decision based on salary, in the existential frame you may be asking yourself questions like: What does money mean to me? If I were older looking back on this decision, would my perception change? Is this kind of work really how I want to be spending my time?

Earlier I referred to *thinking in frames* as a thought process that you cycle through because once you've considered each frame, you move back down through the frames (or hop around as needed). In thinking about the situation in the existential frame, say you come to understand that you don't want money to drive the decision (and can afford to make that choice), and what you really want to prioritize is creating as much control over your time as you can. That's a different problem to solve than finding a job that pays a certain amount. It invites different tradeoffs and sacrifices into the decision and different ways of thinking about your work, and perhaps your career. It insists on different actions that may need to be taken at the pragmatic level.

Perhaps you need to start looking for jobs in a different industry or in a different city. Perhaps you need to go back to school to gain the knowledge and skills needed to pursue the type of work that will best allow you to fulfill the goals you're aligning around.

You can also apply the degrees of freedom thinking at the existential level, which can help shape how you perceive situations and decisions at lower levels as well. You may come to understand that where you live deeply influences how you feel. Maybe that's living close to family, maybe that's living in the country and feeling close to nature. Those kinds of observations about yourself can help you establish pivot points around which you can consider alternatives that remain in line with what you know you need to flourish.

It's not any one frame that provides the useful information, so much as the movement between them that can offer new perspective and refreshed insight. It's getting clear on the plane of action on which you currently sit, identifying your degrees of freedom, then shifting into the strategic and existential frames to start evaluating and questioning those parts of the decision framework you've created.

CAREER QUESTIONS AND LEADERSHIP

I think it's a fair question at this moment to wonder what this line of thinking has to do with leadership.

Consider, you're reading a book about developing your mindset as a leader, which means you're thinking about your career. You're thinking about how to get more effective at your work, how to advance, how to have a more intentional impact on the people around you, and looking for things in this book that may help you. This pursuit is intimately bound up in who you are and the extent to which you view yourself as capable of leading. The way you show up to other people, especially to those people you may be leading, is shaped by what you believe is important and worthwhile and possible. It is shaped by what you're trying to accomplish and how deeply you've thought about your answer to that question.

What do your goals represent?

To revisit the earlier idea, your work may very intentionally be the thing that you're prioritizing in your life and the thing that you believe is most important. This is not necessarily good or bad, but the trouble comes when you make that choice in an unexamined way, that's when it can lead to unintended consequences for you and the people around you. For example, a somewhat common (albeit slightly absurd) situation I encounter in coaching is the startup founder whose response to *what are you trying to accomplish?* is something like, "I want to grow my company, sell it, and make a hundred million dollars." Again, not necessarily a good or bad goal, but certainly an interesting one.

What's interesting about it is that it's representative of underlying values (or at least what's being valued at the moment), and likely several other underlying objectives. An answer like this immediately makes me wonder – what's the goal beneath the goal? Maybe it's obtaining a sense of financial security ("I don't want to have to think about money."), maybe it's an artifact of a strong competitive drive ("Money is how you keep score and I want to win."), or an association between money and status ("If I'm wealthy people will respect me more."), or the desire to prove something ("I'll show them."), etc.

Now, let's use the *hundred-million-dollar-goal* as a proxy for wherever your mind first went when you read the question, "What are you trying to accomplish?" Yours may not be quite so money-centric, but whatever it is, it's acting as a symbol of some underlying goals or needs. Do you know what they are? Those needs you're trying to meet that often go unrecognized and unspoken, the ones that slosh around in your interactions with others and impact how you show up and make decisions.

How do your goals impact what you do?

Stick with this hundred-million-dollar-goal for a moment longer, and let's consider it using the *thinking in frames* model. At the pragmatic level, let's say this goal represents a drive for financial security, essentially, *I want enough money to not have to worry about money anymore*. At the strategic level, you may imagine that having that much money will allow you to do the things you *really* want to do. Maybe that's pursuing other business ideas that require some amount of capital, maybe it's doing a type of work that isn't as lucrative, or simply wanting not to have a boss.

This is useful, because now we're starting to understand that it may not be the money itself that's solving the problem, but the circumstances the money might enable. Then, at the existential level, you start to consider that achieving this goal is really in service of having more time to pursue other interests, hobbies that have been on your to-do list, but never seem to rise to the proper level of importance. What's useful about where we are now is that we've moved from "I want to make a hundred million dollars" to "really I just want more time for my hobbies."

I know that this is an overly simplistic example, but consider in this case that the stated goal is likely directly impeding the expression of the underlying desire. The amount of time and effort it requires to generate that amount of wealth almost certainly precludes time for anything else at the everyday level.

LEADERSHIP AND CAREER QUESTIONS

There's a truism in helping professions that goes like this: *Hurt people hurt people.* It conveys the idea that people who have experienced pain or trauma are more likely to inflict the same on others, either as a defense mechanism or because they replicate patterns of behavior they have endured. In coaching, I think of it like this: *How do you strive without the engine of your striving making you (and everyone around you) miserable?*

In his book *On Becoming a Leader*, Warren Bennis says, "the difference between desire and drive is the difference between expressing yourself and proving yourself."[4] If you don't examine your career goals, if you don't interrogate them and develop some understanding of what you're trying to accomplish in life and why, you won't *really* know what's driving you. You won't know what you're trying to prove, and you will struggle to tap into a way of leading that comes from that most natural place within you. You will struggle to find a truly sustainable and energizing way of expressing yourself, acting on your ideas, and inviting others to join you.

The purpose of giving you a tool like *thinking in frames* is to help you gain perspective on yourself, pressure test different courses of action, and tune into the underlying motives that may be at play in complex decision situations. It provides an access point at the everyday level to your greatest existential interests/concerns. Use it to develop some clarity around what you're trying to accomplish and to gain a clearer understanding of what it is that you're after in wanting to lead other people.

Key questions and takeaways

1. **What are you trying to accomplish in your life?**
   a. The intersection of professional ambitions and life's overarching goals highlights the indivisible nature of work and life. Clarity in your professional objectives not only shapes your career trajectory but also influences your overall sense of purpose and fulfillment.
2. **What are the degrees of freedom that you work around in your career?**
   a. Considering how your values and beliefs shape your goals can be a useful way to gain some clarity on what the less moveable pieces of your career decision-making equation are. This can make it easier to make decisions, and potentially to discern the motive that leading others is aiming to fill.
3. **In what ways do your professional objectives reflect your broader life goals?**
   a. How well do you understand your motivations and natural inclinations toward leading others? Carry the question around in the back of your mind today and see what insights emerge. Jot down a few ideas so you can consider them later.

NOTES

1 Christensen, Clayton M. "How will you measure your life." *Harvard Business Review* 88, no. 7/8 (2010): 46–51.
2 Cukier, Kenneth, Viktor Mayer-Schönberger, and Francis de Véricourt. *Framers: Human advantage in an age of technology and turmoil.* Penguin (2022).
3 Becker, Ernest. *The denial of death.* The Free Press (1973).
4 Bennis, Warren G. *On becoming a leader.* Basic Books (1990), 123.

CHAPTER 6

What do you owe the people you lead?

Not long ago, I was eating chicken wings with a client talking about the recent unwinding of his company. A few months prior, he had been a CEO, leading a team, and trying to grow into new markets. We had started meeting because he had become apprehensive about the future of his business, fearing that the market was cooling and worried that this fear was causing him to lead differently. His team was operating from a place of uncertainty, they wanted to do whatever they could to keep the company going, but they also wondered whether they should be searching for new jobs instead. His anxiety was showing up at work and at home, a little less open-minded with his team, a little sharper with his wife and kids.

When the company ultimately failed, he felt a lot of things, but when really pushed, when he really tried to dig into everything that was going on, what he felt was a sense of relief. All his professional goals had been oriented around the desire to be the CEO of a company. An unexamined assumption he'd had growing up caused him to believe that the trajectory of his career would basically be this: go to college, get a job, diligently work his way up the hierarchy until he became the CEO of a company, then retire and serve on boards. It wasn't an explicit goal exactly, but it was a subconscious narrative that shaped his professional identity. He was progressing, or he wasn't; he was on track, or he wasn't. In an executive assessment earlier in his career, he'd been asked if his aspiration was to be the CEO of a company and he had said, "It's not a matter of if, but when." He wanted to be a leader.

DOI: 10.4324/9781032616193-7

In a sense, with the unwinding of his company, he felt he had failed at the very thing he had aspired to his whole career. But in retrospect, he hadn't much enjoyed the job. There were parts of his work that he'd really enjoyed on his way to the top spot. He enjoyed the analysis, taking a deep dive into a certain market, running numbers on investment opportunities and thinking about where and how to deploy capital in the most strategic way. He'd also enjoyed teaching others how to think in the same way.

As CEO, he hadn't made any time to mentor others, finding himself feeling overwhelmed by the uncertainty he was managing on behalf of the business. He had a mentor's sensibility that came out when he was engaged in the work, but he never really invested much attention into that interest because he was always on the march to the next step of his career. Many of our coaching conversations centered around this drive, to be the one in charge, to get to the top job. Where had it come from, what had fueled it, and what could be made of that drive now that he was no longer in that position?

Eventually, he did something that not many former CEOs do, he took a job working for someone else, managing a smaller team. He decided to go back to the kind of role he had had before making the jump into the top job, focusing on the work that he had enjoyed doing during the day, building a team of people he enjoyed working with and whom he felt he could help develop in their own careers.

THE PUSH INTO MANAGEMENT

It is an unfortunate reality that in most organizations today, the only way to advance is to move into a management role. Typically, people who are promoted into these roles first excel as individual contributors. Take your best faculty member, make them the head of the department. Find your best engineer, give them an engineering team to lead. Pluck your best salesperson from the top of the list, put them in charge of a sales team.

It's not that this never works, but it's a challenging talent strategy because doing a job is different from managing people who do that job. Managing a sales or engineering team is different work than doing sales or engineering; being an effective faculty member requires a different skillset than being an effective administrator. From a career standpoint, the problem is that moving up is how we tend to gain more income, more visibility, more prestige. In many companies, the implicit assumption is that you either move up or, eventually, you move out.

What this does in our organizations is not only incentivize ambitious people to move into roles they may not be interested in for the sake of advancing their careers but it also encourages them to give up skills and interests that may really energize them at work. It's as if we've created a trap where being capable at a certain type of work means that you'll eventually ride that capability into leadership.

This can be unfortunate because, as we've discussed, leading people is a different type of work. It's a task with a different day-to-day rhythm, it's fundamentally social, it's relational. The degree of interaction with others that leading requires may change from industry to industry, or from one organization to another, but at its core, leadership is for people.

Do you enjoy working with people? Do you want to spend more of your time listening to what's going on in other people's lives and helping them navigate it? Do you want to help other people understand, stay committed, and get better at their work? What do you want to spend your time doing on a day-to-day basis? Do you want to lead? It's ok if you do. It's ok if you don't.

Let me tell you something, *Ross the Leader* wants to lead. He wants to be charged up and dialed in and ready to take on all the uncertainty, complexity, and responsibility that leading entails. He wants to be capable of all things and uncertain in none. Aware, prepared, magnetic. *Ross the Leader* wants to rise to the challenge at hand. And yet, I know that I'm not that person. I am uncertain. My confidence ebbs and flows. I have questions. I like the craft of what I do. In general, I'm more interested in spending my time doing coaching and consulting than I am in managing coaches and consultants.

There's a reader in my mind who encounters the questions above and thinks something like *if I'm honest, what I really want to do on a day-to-day basis is just play golf.* I understand that inclination. I identify with it (even though my chosen hobby probably wouldn't be golf – what would yours be?). If that's where your mind goes when you're reading this, I'd encourage you to interrogate that thought. Is leading other people the right goal? Do you want to lead, or do you want the imprimatur of a leadership position? Have you fully considered why you're doing what you're doing; what you want to accomplish?

These are important questions to ask yourself because your answers don't exist in a vacuum.

YOU ARE HAVING AN IMPACT

The idea of you and your work having an impact is not a question, it is a fact. It's not a matter of getting to the point where you're impacting others or rising to the proper level. I think this may be one of the most important insights a person can develop as they learn about leadership and who they are as a leader. If you are in a role that requires leading, *you are impacting the people around you.* Whether you're mindful of that impact, whether you're intentional about trying to shape the impact you have, whether the impact you're having is positive or negative, those are all open questions. But the fact of impact is not.

You are in a leadership relationship with the people in your organization, the people on your team, the people who report to you, the people who have decided to follow you. They may look up to you, they may look to you for support, guidance, permission, acceptance; they may love you and they may hate you. The things you do, the things you say, the way you say them, the decisions you make, they all have direct and indirect effects on these people.

The people you lead carry your impact with them into their own relationships, into their own leadership, their teams, their friendships, their families. They carry your impact with them on their commute at the end of the day, and when they get home at night and set down their keys, the things you do and say to them daily are on their minds and are a part of the conversations they have with loved ones at the dinner table. In this way, the impact of your leadership suffuses itself into the world beyond your organization. Think of it as the leadership commons, the way your behavior as a leader ripples out through the relationships of the people you're leading.

What kind of impact are you having? Are you grinding people down or building them up? Are you holding them accountable by letting them know only when they fall short, or giving them feedback, showing them how to improve, and teaching them how to excel? Are you infusing positivity or injecting negativity into the leadership commons? This is not to say you're responsible for other people's behavior or mental health, exactly, but it is worth considering what level of responsibility you bear for how you impact others.

All of this raises a few important and challenging questions, and I believe the point of these questions is to ask them, not necessarily to answer them: To what extent are you responsible for the people you lead? What do you owe them?

I'm not sure there is one right answer. There are entire philosophical lines of inquiry related to questions like these.[1] To the extent that you can arrive at an answer for yourself, it is likely heavily informed by your own ethics, morals, and theology. Suffice it to say, leading is a task that is interwoven with responsibility for other people and one that leaves a mark.

WHAT WILL YOU LEAVE BEHIND?

Legacy is the word we use to describe the far-reaching effects of events, endeavors, thoughts, and behaviors. We talk about legacy at every possible level, from the wildly abstract to the concrete; from the global to the local, from groups to families to individual relationships. You might consider the legacy of the enlightenment, of folk music; of a sports team or a work of art; a public official or a company founder; a long deceased relative, a family member, or a dear friend.

Legacy is all around us because a question about legacy is a question about the long-lasting impact of something; it is how we try to evaluate and understand the impression that has been left on others or the world around us. It is how we contemplate the mark we might leave.

I love talking to leaders about legacy because it immediately sets the conversation in the future looking back. It is a way of stepping out of the present moment to consider the possible far-reaching effects of what you're doing, of how you're leading. What kind of legacy do you imagine you're building right now? It's a new angle in the conversation, a consideration of what you're trying to accomplish at the largest possible scale, an invitation to the big unwieldy questions that prime the mind for perspective taking: "What is this all for?" "What will be left of all this when I'm gone?"

Ok, I know this is all sounding a bit grandiose, and perhaps the idea of thinking about your legacy seems like a bit of a reach. How much do you really control your legacy after all? A legacy is inherently what's left behind. It's a bit like asking how much control you have over your own reputation. Your reputation is made up of the beliefs and perceptions that other people have about you. To the extent you have any control over your reputation, it is only by way of your behavior. If, on a day-to-day basis, you show up for meetings five minutes early, eventually you will develop a reputation as someone who is never late. If you consistently show up and try at something, even when the showing up and trying is hard, you will eventually develop a reputation as someone who never gives up.

Legacy, as grandiose as the term can be, operates in the same way. We don't control what we leave behind except insofar as we can control our day-to-day behavior. It is in these everyday interactions that our impact on others is formed in ways both small and big. In the same way that our attention accumulates and becomes our patterns of behavior, the impact we have on others accumulates too and becomes our legacy.

A LEGACY OF EVERYDAY LEADERSHIP

I want to tell you about a leader who had this kind of impact on me. He managed a small team and had some specific ideas about what he wanted working with him to feel like. Occasionally, he spoke about it directly, his desire to build community, to collaborate, and to enhance the well-being of his team and clients alike, but mostly he acted on these ideas on a daily basis.

He refused to get to the office earlier than 8:30 AM, and each day he closed his computer at 4:30 PM, aiming to walk out of the office by 5 PM. He didn't do this because he wasn't busy or didn't feel the pressure of all the work he and his team had to get done, but because he had a young family, and he knew his team members did too. He didn't say, "prioritize your family," but he showed family could be prioritized without penalty.

In this way, he invited the people he led into a reality where the needs of life at the office did not always outrank the needs of life outside the office. He showed that it was ok to have hobbies, to spend time with friends and family, to take vacation. He showed that it was ok to work hard, to be inventive and ambitious, and ok to take breaks.

Each day around 2:30 PM, he would stand up and invite his team to go for a walk to a local coffee shop. It wasn't a requirement, and coffee wasn't the point so much as the mid-afternoon pause. It was as if he was saying, *I know that you're a person in this job, and I believe people need breaks to do their best work.* The effect this behavior had on his team was notable. They chatted causally about projects; they relaxed a bit; they laughed; they enjoyed spending time together.

When people on his team got promoted, they maintained this same kind of leadership posture. They tended to the demands of the work, but also to the demands of the day. His employees found themselves doing the best work of their career. They felt creative and energized and cared for, and that effect seeped out into their lives and relationships, to their colleagues, to their friends, and to their spouses. Spouses like me.

Here's the odd part about this leader, I only spent time with him on a few occasions while my wife worked for him. But I heard stories about him. How he shared his ideas, how he encouraged people, how he got involved in the work and how he responded when things went wrong. I could feel the effect of his leadership through the impact he had on his team. I benefitted indirectly from the legacy of his leadership, and I'm still thinking about it a decade later.

Now, the culture of this firm was unique to the time and the place and industry in which it operated. The specific leadership behaviors here are not exactly the point, so much the inclination to tend to the everyday moment. I'm almost certain this team leader was not thinking about his own legacy at the time; more likely he was thinking about how to deliver for his clients, how to do good work, how to lead his team in the best way he could. But the decisions he made on a daily basis, the ways in which he anticipated, participated, and cooperated with the people around him, had this cumulative effect.

Grand gestures and marquee achievements capture our attention, but the most profound influence we have on the people around us often manifests in the smallest actions.

It's these daily decisions and interactions – sharing our ideas, acting on them, inviting others into what we imagine is possible – that shape the highest aims and the everyday impact of our work as leaders.

Key questions and takeaways

1. **How do the expectations of your organization, or the culture around you, shape your perception of leadership roles?**
   a. People are often nudged into roles that require managing and leading others as a means of career advancement, sometimes at the expense of personal fulfillment and the misalignment of interests. Understanding and questioning these expectations can lead to more meaningful career decisions that align with your personal values and strengths and may ultimately enhance your leadership effectiveness over time.
2. **What do you owe the people you lead?**
   a. Have you ever considered directly what you owe the people you lead? What is the social contract that you're engaging in? Considering the nature of the relationship that you're in with those who fall under the purview of your leadership is a necessary step to becoming a more intentional leader.
3. **How might your approach to leadership be shaping your legacy?**
   a. Our everyday behavior has a profound effect on the people around us, especially when we bear some leadership responsibility for them. In what ways can you aim to leave a lasting, positive mark on the people you work with on a daily basis?

NOTE

1 For example, Scanlon, T.M. *What we owe to each other*. Belknap Press (2000).

Afterword

Now what?

AFTERWORD: NOW WHAT?

At the end of a book on everyday leadership, there is a strong urge to point out the fact that you can tune into the everyday moment right now. You can take that one thought that stuck with you, that one idea or inkling, set the book down, and just go give it a try. I know how hard that can be though, taking the first step. But what if you didn't view that first step as a form of work, but as a form of play?

Work seems to ascribe a certain difficulty and seriousness to the task of leading. *If it was supposed to be fun, they wouldn't call it work*, that's how the cliche goes. Play, on the other hand, invites some winsomeness into the whole idea. Maybe it makes it seem more doable. Maybe you don't need to be as prepared to try.

Thinking about the possibility of leadership as play may be a useful way to shift your mindset. I'm not saying *just go have fun* exactly; not *take it less seriously*, but perhaps *hold it more loosely*. Psychologically, play has some specific parameters, it's: "(a) self-chosen, (b) self-directed, (c) intrinsically motivated, (d) structured by mental rules, and (e) creative."[1] Essentially, you decide what to do and how to do it.

You don't play in the future. You play in the present. You may consider the future, but by-and-large play requires a heightened sense for the here-and-now, for the people around you, for the layout of the field or the situation you're in, and for what others are doing. It is both a proactive and reactive posture.

In some ways, I wonder if the definition of play doesn't capture something essential about what leading is like in the best circumstances. I suppose you could lead effectively if

DOI: 10.4324/9781032616193-8

the task of leadership was not self-chosen; some are chosen by others, or they're obligated to lead in some way. And I suppose it's not necessary that leadership be self-directed or intrinsically motivated either. But imagine you're being led by someone in the absence of these conditions – self-chosen, self-directed, intrinsically motivated – doesn't it raise some questions in your mind about who is leading you and why?

If leadership is only an obligation, I don't think that means it can't be done well, not necessarily. But I do think that sense of obligation – leadership as work – can creep into your leading and weigh it down, sap it of the openness and curiosity that brings new ideas and fuels some of the joy and fun that can be found in this kind of relationship.

If leadership is play, then you're always opting in. You don't have to do it, and because of that, you can try. You don't need to be prepared in the same way. And that's good because the simple fact is this, if you're waiting to lead until you feel fully prepared, you will always be waiting.

Everyone feels like an imposter at some point in their career. At some level, I wonder if there's a part of each of us just waiting to be exposed as a fraud. I believe this an artifact of ongoing learning and growing, of leaning into uncertainty and trying new things. You simply will start leading before you feel fully equipped because part of the equipment you need is acquired on the job.

That's not to say just let those imposter feelings run roughshod over you and get on with it. Talk to other people, invite them in, bring them alongside you for support. Keep learning, keep making the effort. Go get creative with your leadership practice, welcome some discomfort as you learn how to do it, and then how to do it better. Go start tinkering. Play. You may be surprised by the impact you can have.

NOTE

1 Gray, Peter. "When Work Is Play." *Play Makes Us Human* (blog). December 03, 2023. https://petergray.substack.com/p/24-when-work-is-play

Workbook

Putting the book to work

WORKBOOK: PUTTING THE BOOK TO WORK

My hope is that *Everyday Leadership* has sparked some insight about your leadership and your work. As is frequently the problem with these strokes of insight, they can be quite challenging to employ. The question is always how to go from *knowing* to *doing*. To try to help you bridge that gap, I put this workbook together. It brings through some of the questions raised throughout the book and provides space for you to make notes, jot down your thoughts and ideas, and start working through how to apply them in your own life and work.

The exercises and questions that follow are generally arranged by how the ideas are presented in the book and are organized to correspond with each chapter. The workbook is designed for each question to be answered in an individual journaling format; however, the exercises are equally useful in sparking group discussions around topics such as leadership, career development, team dynamics, and organizational culture.

For more information about how to use *Everyday Leadership* with your team or organization, visit: https://www.everyday-leadership.com/

EXERCISE A: WHO YOU ARE IS HOW YOU LEAD

The introduction of the book guides readers through the mental transition into leadership, offering a perspective that you must learn how to lead as yourself, not by becoming some new person. It encourages readers to develop their own leadership

DOI: 10.4324/9781032616193-9

approach that resonates with their values and the realities of their professional environment. Accordingly, these exercises are designed to help you develop more awareness and understanding of the circumstances that are bringing you to this book and what you are hoping to take away from it.

A. What kind of changes are you navigating in your work? Are you going through a transition of some kind? What are you adjusting to?

	Example:
	• A way to think about leadership that feels relevant to my daily life • Feel less like an imposter • Just enjoy reading about leadership

B. What is making you most uncomfortable about your work right now?

	Example:
	Recently got promoted into a new role and just trying to get my arms around what I need to be doing in order to be successful

C. List the three to five things you are hoping to get out of reading this book. What problems are you trying to solve?

	Example:
	I've never led a team before
	OR
	My company is growing so fast it feels like every time I'm getting up to speed everything changes again

Exercise 1: What we talk about when we talk about leadership

Chapter 1 aims to get you thinking about leadership in a way that extends beyond traditional archetypes to a broader, more inclusive understanding. The first step in doing that is reflecting on your preexisting notions and questioning some of your beliefs about what leadership is (or needs to be). The goal is to help you parse through your implicit theories of leadership and emphasizes the importance of recognizing effective leadership behavior in day-to-day interactions over extraordinary events or endeavors. These exercises will help you (and your team) start to break down and articulate the ideas and assumptions that are already shaping your perceptions of what it means to lead. This process allows you to understand your preconceived notions and start to question them – What ideas are still useful? What might be to reconsider or throw out entirely?

1. Off the top of your head, jot down the first thing you think about when you think about leadership:

	Example: I think a company founder OR I think about a teacher I had in High School

1.1. When you think of the word "leader" **who** comes to mind?

	Example: A boss I had early in my career OR My professor in graduate school

1.2. What do leaders do?

Example:

They can see and explain things that I cannot see or explain in the same way, they are willing and able to share that perspective with me in a way that helps me

1.3. What do leaders *not* do?

Example:

For better or worse, I find myself thinking that a leader is never only interested in their own well-being

1.4. What does it mean to be leaderlike?

	Example:
	Shaping perceptions and the course of events

1.5. What makes a leader great?

	Example:
	Greatness implies some sense of grandeur that I think can be misleading
	OR
	Being able to unite people

1.6. What do you think makes a leader effective? List the first three to five things that come to mind.

	Example:
	• Taking time to talk and listen to others • Communicating in a way that inspires others • Knowing when to grind and when to rest

1.7. What do you think makes a leader effective **in your organization**? List the first three to five things that come to mind.

	Example:
	• Knowing the products backwards and forwards • Working long hours • Being social

1.8. On a scale of 1–10, circle the number that you think best represents **your current effectiveness** as a leader:

1	2	3	4	5	6	7	8	9	10

| Entirely ineffective | | | Moderately ineffective | | Moderately effective | | | Extremely effective | |

Consider the number you circled, and answer the following two questions in turn:

1.9. Why did you not rate your effectiveness one number **lower**?

	Example: I do a good job of staying in touch with my team and helping them navigate challenges

1.10. Why did you not rate your effectiveness one number **higher**?

	Example: I could do a better job of communicating the vision of the organization in a simpler, more inspiring way

1.11. What are your "subjunctive oughts?" When do you think to yourself, "I *should* be doing XYZ," or "I *should* be leading in XYZ way?" What type of action is "the should" suggesting?

	Example:
	I should be better at coaching my team
	OR
	I should be helping my employees sell more

1.12. When you think of **event-driven leadership,** a person stepping up in challenging circumstances and saying or doing just the right thing, what/who do you think about?

	Example:
	I think of the president standing on the rubble at the twin towers with a bullhorn.
	OR
	I wonder if I would/ could be that person if/when the event occurs. Do I have what it takes?

1.13. When you think of **endeavor-driven leadership,** a person leveraging their unrelenting drive for success in some venture, what/who do you think about?

	Example:
	Community minded leaders taking on generations-long challenges to drive positive change in their cities
	OR
	I think of RJ Scaringe building a new EV company

1.14. When you think of **everyday leadership,** a person engaged in the act of leading others on a day-to-day basis, what/who do you think about?

	Example:
	My boss asking me about my vacation with genuine interests while checking in on work progress
	OR
	I think of someone who is dedicated to the daily process of trying to make something great; someone who just keeps showing up

Exercise 2: What a leader does

Chapter 2 aims to help you redefine leadership, helping you think of it as a universal, behavior-based activity, rather than a phenomenon that is reserved for select individuals or people in certain positions. The essential elements of leadership – anticipation, participation, and cooperation – are presented as a way of understanding how the practice of leadership is embedded in the simple acts of everyday life. It also provides some of the research background behind leadership behavior as a way of breaking down your own individual inclinations (Do you prefer more relationship, task, or change-oriented behavior?), as well as the demands of your role (Does your role demand more relationship, task, or change-oriented behavior?). Ultimately, it is an encouragement to embrace your own potential for leading without needing to fit some preexisting model or method. The exercises in this section aim to help you break down elements of your own thinking applying these lenses to gain some perspective on your own preferences, development needs, and the demands of your environment.

2. When you think of the fundamental principles behind what leadership accomplishes – anticipation, participation, and cooperation – what behaviors come to mind that you do/see on a daily basis?

> Example:
>
> Community minded leaders taking on generations-long challenges to drive positive change in their cities
>
> OR
>
> I think of RJ Scaringe building a brand new EV company

2.1. What parts of your work require anticipation, participation, and cooperation?

Anticipation	Participation	Cooperation

Example:

- Creating a marketing strategy
- Setting a hiring plan
- Managing finances

Example:

- Writing marketing copy
- Interviewing candidates
- Writing checks

Example:

- Getting the marketing team excited about the strategy
- Coordinating interviews with other team members
- Getting everyone to stick to the budget

2.2. List out the activities and responsibilities that represent your work. Don't overthink the task, relationship, and change categories just yet, just start listing activities.

Activity/Responsibility	Relationship	Task	Change
	☐	☐	☐
	☐	☐	☐
	☐	☐	☐
	☐	☐	☐
	☐	☐	☐
	☐	☐	☐
	☐	☐	☐
	☐	☐	☐
	☐	☐	☐
	☐	☐	☐
	☐	☐	☐
	☐	☐	☐
Setting the strategy for the marketing group	☐	☐	X
Bringing the team together to work toward a common goal	X	☐	☐
Writing reports	☐	X	☐

2.3. Keeping in mind the following ideas from Chapter 2:

- **Relationship-oriented** leader behaviors focus on establishing, maintaining, and improving interpersonal relationships.
- **Task-oriented** leader behaviors orient people toward the accomplishment of goals.
- **Change-oriented** leader behaviors are those that help people adapt, evolve, and see what could be.

Now, go back through your list and check which box you think **primarily** represents the leadership behavior you're employing when you're doing that activity. Then, add the checks in each column

2.4. What does this exercise teach you about your role? What percentage of your role does each category of leadership behavior represent?

	Example:
	So many of the things I do are very task-oriented
	OR
	So much of my role is change-oriented, but I don't enjoy that type of work

2.5. What changes could you make to the percentage of leader behavior to be more effective in your role?

Example:

Spending more time on relationship-oriented behavior might help me drive results on a larger scale

OR

Maybe I could hire someone to take on the change-oriented work so I can focus on what I'm best at

Exercise 3: How the task of leadership evolves

Chapter 3 shows how the task of leadership evolves as your purview changes and as organizations grow and evolve. It highlights the need to acknowledge the changing time horizon of your work, transition from direct control to more strategic influence, manage expanding responsibilities, and confront the uncertainties of change. Accordingly, the questions in this section aim to help you break down your understanding of your role, thinking about its time horizon, how you think about balancing control and influence, and your perception and management of the reality of uncertainty.

3. What is the time horizon of the tasks you're working on?
    Is the time horizon of your role changing?

	Example:
	In the past it would take ~6 months to close a deal, but now the time horizon of my role isn't as clear
	OR
	Managing more people has changed how much time it takes for me to be effective in my role

3.1. What impact might a changing time horizon be having
     on how you perceive your productivity and effectiveness?

	Example:
	We don't know if we've made a good hire until their second year
	OR
	It may take 5 years to know whether this strategy was a good idea or not

3.2. What does the timeline of your work tell you about the balance between control and influence in your role?

> Example:
>
> I'm having to rely on a lot more people to get things done at this level
>
> OR
>
> I'm having to delegate the shorter term tasks, which makes it much less clear to me when I've had a productive day

3.3. What is your relationship to the uncertainty in your role? What do you do to manage uncertainty and ambiguity?

> Example:
>
> Uncertainty tends to make me anxious, so when I start feeling anxious about work, I try to focus on short-term tasks that I know build toward our long-term goals
>
> OR
>
> I have a group of peers I talk to about all the uncertainty we're facing, which helps keep it in perspective

Exercise 4: Learning how you practice leadership

Chapter 4 is a nudge to start considering your natural tendencies toward people and tasks, to seek feedback to help you better understand your strengths and weaknesses. It is an encouragement to experiment with new behaviors, remain curious, and embrace discomfort in the interest of learning and growth. To that end, the questions here aim to draw out your understanding of your motives, values, and preferences. The goal of exercises like these is to build self-awareness and develop a language and framework for thinking about where and how you spend your time, and how that can shape your effectiveness.

4. What do you enjoy doing? What are your interests? List three to five interests below.

Example:

- Reading
- Trail running
- Talking to people about their work
- Writing

4.1. What kinds of tasks tend to give you energy and hold your attention?

	Example:
	• Reading something interesting
	• Trying to get a sentence or paragraph just right
	• Coming up with new ideas

4.2. What kind of behavior comes naturally to you? What kinds of things do people tend to notice or compliment you about?

	Example:
	• I'm a good communicator
	• I'm dedicated to my business
	• I help other people succeed

4.3. What do you spend your time doing during the day? Think about your average week, look at your calendar and count up the hours for how you spend your time. How would you categorize those activities behaviorally?

Relationship	Task	Change

Example:

- 1:1s with my direct reports
- Taking clients golfing

Example:

- Editing documents
- Sending out invoices

Example:

- Reading about new technology
- Evaluating how changing market dynamics may impact my business

4.4. Can't think of anything? Ask someone else what they observe (e.g., boss, peers, team, spouse, friends); see if it changes how you perceive yourself.

Example:

My team said they see me making more client calls than I realized, and that they'd like me around to help coach them more often

4.5. What kinds of behavior does your environment demand? What do you need to do to be successful in your role?

Relationship	Task	Change

Example:
- Lots of meetings with other people
- Drinks and dinners with the board

Example:
- Signing off on end of year employee reviews
- Putting docs together to report to the board

Example:
- Communicating a vision to the team to keep them inspired and moving the same direction

4.6. Imagine you stepped back from your role and were coaching someone else to take over for you. What are the top three things you would tell them they need to do to be most successful?

Example:

- Have direct conversations with the team
- Don't assume everyone knows the vision
- Make decisions quickly and keep moving

4.7. In Chapter 4, you read that your values are your beliefs about what's most important in life, and that your values shape your attention. Consider the following list of 50 values in answering the questions that follow:

Achievement: Personal success according to social standards

Adaptability: The ability to adjust to new conditions

Altruism: Selfless concern for the well-being of others

Ambition: Hard work and striving

Authority: Lead or commanding others

Beauty: Appreciation for aesthetics and the arts

Benevolence: Friendly, generous, and considerate of others

Broad-mindedness: Tolerance and acceptance of different ideas and beliefs

Caring: Showing compassion and concern for others

Cautiousness: Being careful to avoid potential problems or dangers

Cleanliness: Maintaining order and cleanliness in one's surroundings

Collaboration: Working effectively with others

Commitment: Dedication to a cause or activity

Competence: Doing something successfully or efficiently

Consistency: Reliability and uniformity in actions

Contentment: Satisfaction with one's situation in life

Cooperation: Working together for a common purpose

Courage: Bravery in the face of challenges

Courtesy: Politeness and good manners

Creativity: Thinking outside the box and being imaginative

Curiosity: Interest in and pursuit of knowledge and experiences

Dependability: Being reliable and trustworthy

Dignity: Maintaining self-respect and the respect of others

Empathy: Understanding and sharing the feelings of others

Equality: Equal opportunity and treatment for all

(Continued)

4.10. Now, read through the list again. Based on how you're spending your time on a daily and weekly basis right now, what are you most **valuing** in your everyday life?

Example:

- Self-discipline
- Ambition
- Dependability
- Caring
- Self-discipline

4.11. In what ways do your core values, and what you're valuing most in your everyday life exist in tension or in harmony? What kinds of things might you do to better align them?

Example:

The stress of my work and how I perceive the importance of deadlines is causing me to not prioritize my core values in the way I'd like to

Exercise 5: What are you trying to accomplish?

Chapter 5 widens the aperture of what we're talking about, offering questions about what you hope to achieve and how your professional goals interact with your overarching aims in life. Through "thinking in frames," a technique involving taking pragmatic, strategic, and existential perspectives in considering decisions and ideas, you're encouraged to reflect deeply on your motivations and how your decisions shape your practice of leadership. The questions in this section follow the same logic with the goal of helping you draw out and articulate what you're trying to accomplish at the deepest and broadest level so you can start to understand how that ambition shapes how you show up as a leader.

5. If someone asked you, *what are you trying to accomplish?* what would you say to them?

Example:

I'd like to grow my business to a size that would allow me to step back and not be directly involved in day-to-day operations

OR

I'm trying to be the most present parent I can, while still providing for my family

Excitement: Seeking stimulation and thrills

Fairness: Justice and equity in treatment and decisions

Forgiveness: Letting go of grudges and resentment

Freedom: Autonomy and independence

Friendship: Valuing close, supportive relationships

Health: Physical and mental well-being

Helpfulness: Being of service and assistance to others

Honesty: Truthfulness and sincerity

Inner Harmony: Being at peace with oneself

Intellectual Stimulation: Engaging in thought-provoking activities

Loyalty: Faithfulness to friends, family, and groups

Meaning in Life: Having a sense of purpose

National Security: Protection of one's country from external threats

Obedience: Compliance with rules and authority

Personal Development: Continuous self-improvement

Politeness: Showing good manners and respect

Power: Dominance over people and resources

Privacy: Respecting personal boundaries and confidentiality

Respect for Tradition: Upholding cultural, family, or religious customs

Responsibility: Being accountable for one's actions

Self-discipline: Controlling impulses and emotions

Social Justice: Fighting for fairness and equity in society

Social Order: Stability and security within society

Spirituality: Seeking a deeper connection with the sacred or transcendent aspects of life

Wealth: Material prosperity and financial success

4.8. Read through the list above. What are your five **most important** values?

Example:

- Achievement
- Adaptability
- Altruism
- Ambition
- Authority

4.9. What are your five **least important** values?

Example:

- Obedience
- Personal Development
- Politeness
- Power
- Privacy

5.1. Use the *thinking in frames* model from Chapter 5 to consider how you'd answer the question

Pragmatic (in the here-and-now)	Example: In the here-and-now, I'm trying to learn how to more confidently step into my role
Strategic (…in order to)	Example: If I can lead more confidently, I think I'll be able to grow my company faster
Existential (in the end…)	Example: I'd like to be able to provide for my family, but not in a way that distracts me or prevents me from spending time with them and have close personal relationships with my kids

Exercise 6: What do you owe the people you lead?

Chapter 6 is an encouragement to evaluate the conventional path of career advancement and to consider how your definitions of success and leadership shape the impact you have on others. It highlights the impact of leadership on others and the responsibility that comes with it and urges you to reflect on the legacy you'd like to leave behind. These questions are straightforward but can be challenging to answer. They can be useful to talk about with you significant other or your team, as you aim to clarify what you're trying to accomplish.

6. What do you owe the people you lead? What can you do today to honor your responsibility to the people you lead?

Example:

I owe them my absolute undivided attention, at least some of the time

OR

I'm not exactly sure, but I know I owe them something because of the responsibility I carry on their behalf – I'm excited to ask the team

6.1. What is your legacy motivation? What do you want to leave behind when you're gone? At your funeral, what do you want people to be thinking and saying about what you did while you were here?

Family	Example: • A spouse and kids who know I loved them • Lots of memories from travel and time spent together
Friends	Example: • Memories of meaningful connection, fun times, and good conversation • Places visited together
Work	Example: • That I helped other people along in their journey • That I contributed to the body of work in my profession

Community	Example:
	• That I participated and used my talents, such as they are, to benefit others • That I cared about the community and spent my time and energy participating in making it better for others
Other	Example:
	• I'd like to create some cultural artifacts for others to interact with • I'd like to dedicate myself to an artform later in life

Exercise B: Now what?

The afterword is a direct encouragement to go embrace the opportunities for leading that are right in front of you, even if you feel unprepared or like an imposter. The exercise is a push to go ahead and get your ideas on paper and pick one to act on.

D. What are **seven things you might do next?** Seven things you might do next is a way to articulating the ideas that you may be considering for yourself in the back of your mind. Push beyond the second or third idea and try to get to seven. Get the ideas out on paper so you can see them and evaluate them. What are the realistic practices, opportunities, and potential actions in front of you? What might you actually do? What can you change?

Examples:

- Share my idea for re-organizing my group
- Schedule 1:1's with each member of my team
- Block time each week to read something new
- Start taking my kids to school in the morning
- Research my business idea and start putting together a business plan
- Take 5 minutes each morning to write my ideas down
- Stop working for the day and go for a run

Index

Note: Page numbers followed by "n" refer to notes.

3D printing 27–28

achievement 4, 15, 23, 34, 77, 104
anticipation 26–27, 91–92
anxiety 1, 6–7, 9, 44–45, 70
archetypes 14–15
Assessing CEOs and Senior Leaders: A Primer for Consultants (Blankenship) 7
attention 49, 53–56, 76, 77

behaviors 31–36, 49, 54–57; abusive 32; background 31–32; change-oriented 35–36; ethical 32; and legacy 75–76, 78; passive 32; relationship-oriented 33–34; shapes culture 56–57; task-oriented 34–35
beliefs 14–18, 22, 83; crossed wires 15; images/myths/archetypes 14–15; implicit theories 15–17; subjunctive ought 17–18
Bennis, Warren G. 68, 69n4
Big Five personality traits 32, 38n4
bosses, tale of 5–7
business 4–5, 7, 11, 26–27, 39–40, 51, 60, 70–71

career 12, 48, 64–69, 70–72, 77–78, 110; decisions 64–65; goals 9, 36, 62, 66–68; and leadership 66–68
CEOs 7–8, 21, 25–26, 33, 70–71
change-oriented behavior 35–36, 93–94; *see also* behaviors

Chief Executive Officer *see* CEOs
Christensen, Clayton M. 60–61, 69n1
Churchill, Winston 14
coaching 5, 7, 9, 33, 36, 60–61, 66, 68, 71, 73; *see also* leader/leadership
collaboration 4, 33, 104
commitment 16, 104
communication skill 32, 38n4
company *see* organization
competency models 33–35
control and influence 42–43, 45, 97
cooperation 28–29, 91–92, 104
creativity 52, 104
crossed wires 15
culture 16, 19, 56–57, 77, 81
curiosity 20, 51–52, 104

degrees of freedom 62, 64, 65, 69; *see also* frame/framing

e-commerce store 26
effective leadership 37, 41–42, 45, 51, 57, 83, 88
elements of leadership 26–31, 37; anticipation 26–27; cooperation 28–29; participation 27–28
empathy 34, 104
empowerment 16
endeavor-driven leadership 19–20, 90
engineering 20, 71–72
entrepreneurs 4, 20
environment demands 7, 35–37, 49–50, 91

event-driven leadership 19, 89
everyday leadership 21–22,
    25–37, 76–78, 90; behaviors
    of 31–36; elements of 26–31,
    37; legacy of 75–78, 111;
    principles 36–37
existential frame 64–65, 109;
    see also frame/framing

feeling *vs.* doing 2–3
frame/framing 61–65, 67–68,
    108–109; aim of 62; degrees
    of freedom 62, 64, 65, 69;
    existential 64–65; pragmatic
    62–63; strategic 63–64
friendships 74, 105

goals 66–68; career 9, 36, 62, 66–68;
    impact of 67–68; represent
    66–67
"Great Man" theory 14
greatness 13–14

Harvard Business School 60–61,
    69n1
health 74, 105
How I Built This (podcast) 20,
    24n9
"How Will You Measure Your Life"
    (Christensen) 60–61, 69n1

images 14–15
implicit theories 15–17
individual leadership 6, 18

job change 63–64

King, Martin Luther, Jr. 13

leader/leadership: accomplish
    59–69, 108–109; attention of
    53–56; behaviors 31–36, 49,
    56–57; beliefs 14–18; business
    4–5, 39–40; career questions
    and 66–68; challenges in 3–4,
    31, 49–50; competency models
    33–35; details 29–31; do/don't
    do 12–13, 85; effective 37,

41–42, 57; emergence of 16,
    19, 87; as empowerment 16;
    as entrepreneurial spirit
    20; environment 49–50;
    everyday 21–22, 25–37, 91–95;
    feeling *vs.* doing 2–3; form
    of interaction 4; form of play
    79–80; fundamental elements of
    26–31; impact of 73–74; implicit
    theories 15–17; individual 6, 18;
    introduction 1–10; learning
    and practicing 47–57, 98–107;
    levels 18–19, 43; making great
    13–14, 86; and management 15,
    23n2, 32, 71–73; means to 13, 86;
    natural 49–51; organizational
    3–4, 18–19, 35–36, 43–44, 54,
    73–74; owe the people 70–78,
    110–111, 110–112; perceptions 2,
    4, 10, 19–20, 23, 78; positions 15,
    25, 47, 49; preconceived notions
    of 12–14; principles 36–37; and
    psychological concepts 15, 21;
    skills 2, 32, 72; talk about 11–23,
    83–90; task evolution of 39–45,
    95–97; theories of 4, 14, 15–17, 53;
    transformational 35; values of
    53–54; work of 28–29, 32–34,
    40–44, 77–78
learning/practicing leadership
    47–57, 98–107; behaviors 31–36,
    49, 54–57; comfortable 52–53;
    creativity 52; curiosity 51–52;
    environment demands for
    49–50; natural tendencies for
    48–49; tasks 50–51
legacy 75–78, 111–112
levels, leadership 18–19, 43;
    endeavor 19–20, 90; event 19,
    89; everyday 21–22, 25–37, 90;
    group 18; individual 6, 18;
    organization 18–19, 54
Lincoln, Abraham 13

management 15, 23n2, 32, 71–73
myths 14–15

natural leadership 49–51

Ohio State Leadership Studies 32, 38n6
On Becoming a Leader (Bennis) 68, 69n4
organization 3–4, 35–36, 43–44, 56, 74; behaviors in 35–36, 42–43; communication in 33; environment of 57; leadership 3–4, 18–19, 35–36, 43–44, 54, 73–74; management 71–73; task evolution in 39–45

participation 27, 91–92
power 7, 15, 21, 42, 62, 105
pragmatic frame 62–63, 109; *see also* frame/framing
preconceived notions 12–14, 22
program coordinator 35–37
psychology/psychological 7, 15, 21, 31, 54, 55, 62, 79; consulting 7, 12, 31; leadership concepts 15, 21; parameters 79–80

Raz, Guy 20, 24n9
relationship-oriented behavior 33–34, 93–94, 100, 102; *see also* behaviors
responsibility 33, 59, 72, 74, 78, 105, 110

sales team 55–56
self-reflection 48
skills 2, 13, 21, 32, 39, 48, 65, 72; active listening 33; communication 32, 38n4; creativity 52, 104; feedback 18,

34, 48–49, 57, 74; management 15, 23n2, 32, 71–73; managing conflict 33; organizational 3–4, 35–36, 43–44, 56, 74; positivity 7, 74; responsibility 33, 59, 72, 74, 78, 105, 110; soft 2–3; team building/development 40, 42, 71
strategic frame 63–64, 109; *see also* frame/framing
stress 3, 59
subjunctive ought 17–18, 89

task evolution 39–45, 95–97; control and influence 42–43; time horizon 40–42; uncertainty effect 43–45
task-oriented behavior 34–35, 93–94, 100, 102; *see also* behaviors
team *see* organization
team building/development 40, 42, 71
technology 27–28
thinking in frames *see* frame/framing
time horizon 40–42, 45, 95–96
transformational leadership 35

uncertainty effect 43–45, 97

values 9, 14, 31, 53–54, 104–107

wealth 68, 105
Wells Fargo 56, 58n6, 58n7
work 28–29, 32–34, 40–44, 47–48, 72, 77–78

For Product Safety Concerns and Information please contact our EU
representative GPSR@taylorandfrancis.com
Taylor & Francis Verlag GmbH, Kaufingerstraße 24, 80331 München, Germany